WINNING THE INVISIBLE WAR WITH CHRIST

AKINBOWALE ISAAC ADEWUMI

WINNING THE INVISIBLE WAR WITH CHRIST

AKINBOWALE ISAAC ADEWUMI

Scripture quotations are taken from the HOLY BIBLE, KING JAMES VERSION

DEDICATION

"Now thanks be unto God, which always causeth us to triumph in Christ, and maketh manifest the savour of his knowledge by us in every place."
- 2 Corinthians 2:14.

To the Almighty God Who delivered me from the grip of Satan and his agents.

TABLE OF CONTENTS

PREFACE

"And there was war in heaven: Michael and his angels fought against the dragon; and the dragon fought and his angels, and prevailed not; neither was their place found any more in heaven. And the great dragon was cast out, that old serpent, called the Devil, and Satan, which deceiveth the whole world: he was cast out into the earth, and his angels were cast out with him" (Revelation 12:7-9).

The fight against Satan is an invisible war and we are continuously engaged in a cosmic battle with him and his cohorts. The battle is not optional; it is real and must be fought. This old serpent beguiled Eve in the Garden of Eden but had his head crushed by the Lord Jesus Christ Who is the solution to the problems of humanity. This victory of Christ belongs to all believers today because we are sitting in the heavenly places - the position of victory - to fight the craftiness, enticement, lies and deception that this enemy always throws at us from time to time. Failure to grasp this reality opens the door of opportunity for this monster to attack us and win. Satan influences the world systems and the way humans think; he works through the mind of human agencies to carry out his nefarious operations. *"For we wrestle not against flesh and blood, but against principalities, against powers, against the rulers of the darkness of this world, against spiritual wickedness in high places"* (Ephesians 6:12).

The schemes of Satan can never be overestimated nor underestimated for any reason, but with the right application of the knowledge acquired about his tactics, every believer in Christ is empowered to have continuous victory over this enemy of human soul in every battle. Satan is not equal in power and authority as God, but he is just as real. Yes, the spiritual battle is real and the origin of invisible war is from Satan. With his empty pride, limited power and short time, he continues to deceive humanity into his onslaught of wickedness. Nevertheless, he has been defeated by Christ. Christian should be more focused on God's ability and power than that of Satan and there is no terrible situation in the life of men that God cannot change by His awesome power.

In view of this, God has also given us spiritual armours to fight the battle and win in order to subdue the kingdom of Satan in this world and set his captives free. Many lives, families, homes, territories, provinces, states and nations are under the influence of Satan and his agents. "And when he was come out of the ship, immediately there met him out of the tombs a man with an unclean spirit, Who had his dwelling among the tombs; and no man could bind him, no, not with chains: Because that he had been often bound with fetters and chains, and the chains had been plucked asunder by him, and the fetters broken in pieces: neither could any man tame him. Always, night and day, he was in the mountains, and in the tombs, crying, and cutting himself with stones. But when he saw Jesus afar off, he ran and worshipped him, and cried with a loud voice, and said,

What have I to do with thee, Jesus, thou Son of the most high God? I adjure thee by God, that thou torment me not. For he said unto him, Come out of the man, thou unclean spirit. And he asked him, what is thy name? And he answered, saying, my name is Legion: for we are many" (Mark 5:2-9).

This man had been tormented by six thousand demons continually both day and night for many years. Satan has put a hold on his life and was ready to destroy him. But his story changed when he had a personal encounter with Jesus Christ. This single experience transformed his life and destiny. Christ's power is awesome and has lordship over Satan and demons. By His word, Jesus commanded the demons to come out of him and he was free instantaneously.

No amount of demons in hell can resist the authority of our Lord and Saviour Jesus Christ. Upon realizing His power and authority over them, the evil spirits left immediately. No matter the situation in your life, whether it is similar to that of the Gadarene demoniac who dwelt among tombs or that the enemy has placed a curse on you or your family to kill your joy and steal your peace which was once enjoyed by your family or it may even be that you are suffering from demonic attacks, I announce to you today that Jesus has come to set the captives free and He will exercise dominion and authority over the power of darkness in your life. "And ye shall know the truth, and the truth shall make you free … If the Son therefore shall make you free, ye shall be free indeed" (John 8:32, 36).

Through Jesus' death on the cross at Calvary, Satan has been defeated and Christ purchased victory for His beloved children. This is the victory that true believers have in Christ. Have you given your life to Jesus, or do you think it's not necessary? No sinner can have victory over sins, Satan and demons without the saving power and blood of Jesus Christ. Above all, no one can see God at the end of their journey on earth without salvation. To have this power today, a sinners need to repent of his sins by confessing them to the Lord Jesus and asking for His forgiveness in order to benefit from the finished work of Jesus.

No power in heaven, on earth and beneath can stand at the mention of the mighty name of Jesus. The believer will recover all that the enemy has taken from him. Hence our God is more dependable than what we think or feel. He has given us the both authority and power over Satan to stand against him and his cohorts. The question comes to you again: On whose side are you? Who are you following or obeying? Are you following Satan directly or indirectly? What shall it profit you if you gain the best gifts, talent, healing, protection, riches, fame as a star and all that the world can afford from Satan and you lose your soul with him in hell?

Have you forgotten God, living without remembering His provision of salvation through Jesus Christ? "Neither is there salvation in any other: for there is none other name under heaven given among men, whereby we must be saved...Jesus saith unto him, I am the way, the truth, and the life: no man cometh unto the Father, but by me" (Acts 4:12; John 14:6). Are you a church goer with hypocritical lifestyle – professing to be a Christian, pastor, prophet and apostle that appeared to be righteous before men but wicked and sinful before God? Are you condemned in your heart for hidden besetting sins of the flesh? Is your heart hardened and your conscience dead?

Are you privately a slave of sin, a helpless tool in the hands of Satan? Are you a liar, an adulterer/adulteress, a fornicator, sorcerer, witch, wizard or necromancer? Are murderer of innocent babies, kids and other fellow men. Are you a secret idol worshipper and an instrument in the hands of the devil who yet appears as a minister of God on the pulpit? Are you a saint in the church on Sunday but a sinner during week at home or elsewhere? You can't have one leg in one of these things mentioned above and the other leg in the church and still claim to be a born-again Christian. Hence religion that makes a mere virtue out of faith in God without a corresponding salvation from sinful practices is nothing but self-delusion and deception. Should you die today, where will you spend your eternity?

Religion does not save a soul, only the blood of Jesus has the power to save and to deliver from the power of Satan. "Neither by the blood of goats and calves, but by his own blood he entered in once into the holy place, having obtained eternal redemption *for us*...And they overcame him by the blood of the Lamb (Jesus, the Lamb of God) and by the word of their testimony; and they loved not their lives unto the death" (Hebrews 9:12; Revelation 12:11).

Remember that our time on earth is short but eternity (with Satan in hell or God in heaven) is endless. What the devil offers to humanity in this world is not free but is temporal with grave consequences. But Christ, the Lamb of God, offers us a free opportunity to full salvation of life eternal and victory if we surrender our lives to Him today and want to win the invisible war from this old time enemy. "Whereas ye know not what shall be on the morrow. For what is your life? It is even a vapour, that appeareth for a little time, and then vanisheth away" (James 4:14). It is like a sea without a bottom, like an ocean without a shore. Short as our life is here on earth, endless will it be in eternity. May God help us to know how to number our days. "For the wages of sin is death; but the gift of God is eternal life through Jesus Christ our Lord... So teach us to number our days, that we may apply our hearts unto wisdom" (Romans 6:23; Psalms 90:12).

Chapter 1

THE ORIGIN OF SATAN
AND HIS DEMONS

There is a need for every believer to have a balanced understanding of Satan and maintain a Scriptural attitude towards his activities and that of his agents. Christians often take either of two extreme positions. Some pretend to be unaware of the existence and operations of Satan and demons. This approach is a seeming denial of the bitter hatred that Satan has consistently manifested towards God and man, the crown of His creation.

Other believers tend to over-magnify the power of Satan to the point that his activities overshadow their consciousness of the power of the Almighty God. Hence it is important to know that the Scriptures contain all that believers need to know on the subject of Satan and his demons' activities. Satan's rebellion and fall marked the beginning of sins and all evil. A third of the angels in Heaven joined Satan's rebellion in a coup d'état and were all driven out by God along with him.

"Thou wast perfect in thy ways from the day that thou wast created, till iniquity was found in thee. By the multitude of thy merchandise they have filled the midst of thee with violence, and thou hast sinned: therefore I will cast thee as profane out of the mountain of God: and I will destroy thee,

O covering cherub, from the midst of the stones of fire. Thine heart was lifted up because of thy beauty, thou hast corrupted thy wisdom by reason of thy brightness: I will cast thee to the ground, I will lay thee before kings, that they may behold thee… And there was in their synagogue a man with an unclean spirit; and he cried out, Saying, let us alone; what have we to do with thee, thou Jesus of Nazareth? art thou come to destroy us? I know thee who thou art, the Holy One of God. And Jesus rebuked him, saying, hold thy peace, and come out of him. And when the unclean spirit had torn him, and cried with a loud voice, he came out of him" (Ezekiel 28:15-17; Mark 1:23-26).

Satan was created as a beautiful, holy, perfect and knowledgeable angel by the Almighty God. He was highly placed above other angels in Heaven to lead them with divine ability of holiness in glorifying God... He was also given free will to choose good or evil but because of pride and rebellion, he chose not to retain the glorious position that God had given him, so, he fell. "How art thou fallen from heaven, O Lucifer, son of the morning! how art thou cut down to the ground, which didst weaken the nations! For thou hast said in thine heart, I will ascend into heaven, I will exalt my throne above the stars of God: I will sit also upon the mount of the congregation, in the sides of the north: I will ascend above the heights of the clouds; I will be like the most High. Yet thou shalt be brought down to hell, to the sides of the pit" (Isaiah 14:12-15).

Hence Lucifer (son of the morning) was cast out of heaven and became Satan (perverted character) with the portion of deceived angels who got involved in rebellion against God. These fallen angels are known as demons or evil spirits (forces). This company of demons now constitutes the armies of the kingdom of darkness with established hierarchies (Ephesians 6:12) that are fulfilling Satan's purposes and programs on earth. They are variously referred to in Scriptures as unclean spirits, evils spirits, demons or devils. Demons are spirit beings that cannot function without a body and they, most especially, prefer to operate in human beings/bodies.

The target areas of demons' occupation in humans are the emotion, will/self-awareness, speech and intelli-gence. Satan decided to duplicate all that are God's own by establishing his kingdom on earth to oppose God and remain the enemy of both God and His saints. Satan and his demons have a definite origin, so they have a sure end, a fact that they themselves are fully aware of. "And when he was come to the other side into the country of the Gergesenes, there met him two possessed with devils, coming out of the tombs, exceeding fierce, so that no man might pass by that way. And, behold, they cried out, saying, what have we to do with thee, Jesus, thou Son of God? art thou come hither to torment us before the time? "(Matthew 8:28-29).

The awareness of this fact prompted Satan to continue in his deceptive ways of luring people into sinful practices that would cause them to end up in the Lake of Fire with him.

But Jesus has come to destroy the works of the devil in your life if only you would allow him to be your Lord and Saviour.

CHARACTERISTICS OF DEMONS

The word 'demon' was not used throughout the King James Version of the Bible. However, it is a variant of 'evil spirit,' 'unclean spirit,' 'foul spirit,' 'devils,' 'spirits of devils,' and 'prince of the devils,' used in the Scriptures as some other Bible versions indicate. So, evil spirits or demons are followers of Satan and they carry out full diabolical activities in loyalty to their master. They are destroyers of good things, spoilers and wicked. They inflict people with physical pain, mental misfortune, failure, hardship, barrenness, mysterious occurrences, temptation to commit sins and engagement in immoral practices. For this reason, "God spared not the angels that sinned, but cast them down to hell, and delivered them into chains of darkness, to be reserved unto judgment (2 Peter 2:14). Their roles and activities in the life of men are horrible and detestable.

They are the spirit of contention at home, church and community (2 Chronicles 15:5-6; Judge 9:22-25); They are lying spirits (1 Kings 22:22-23); Unclean spirits (Matthew 10:1; Zechariah 13:2); Evil spirits (1 Samuel 18:10; 19:9); Seducing spirits (1 Timothy 4:1); Wicked spirits (Luke 11:26); Perverse spirits (Isaiah 19:14); spirit of immorality/whoredoms (Hosea 4:12; 5:4): spirits of depression (1 Samuel 16:14-15;); the spirit of fear (2 Timothy 1:7); the spirit of infirmity (Luke 8:2; 13:10-17); dumb and deaf spirit (Mark 9:25); spirit of disobedience (Ephesians 2:2); antichrist spirit (1 John 4:3). They spread false religions and doctrines (1Timothy 4:1; 2 Timothy 3:13; 2 Peter 2:1); they execute Satan's program (Revelation 16:13-14); they oppose God's plan (Daniel 10:10-14; Ephesians 6:12).

CERTAINTY OF THE INVISIBLE WAR FROM SATAN

The Bible declared that Christians are spiritual wrestlers assigned by God. If God is a man of war, of a truth, His children too will follow suit. "For we wrestle not against flesh and blood, but against principalities, against powers, against the rulers of the darkness of this world, against spiritual wickedness in high places" (Ephesians 6:12). The originator of spiritual war against humanity on earth is Satan. He started it in Heaven when he rebelled against God in his attempt to take over the Kingdom of Heaven.

"And there was war in heaven: Michael and his angels fought against the dragon; and the dragon fought and his angels, and prevailed not; neither was their place found any more in heaven. And the great dragon was cast out, that old serpent, called the Devil, and Satan, which deceiveth the whole world: he was cast out into the earth, and his angels were cast out with him" (Revelation 12:7-9). Satan came to deceive, steal, kill and to destroy. Therefore, he chose to form his own kingdom on earth with his demons, causing all spiritual warfare in the life of men. The main target of Satan is to blindfold the people of this world and hinder their salvation which Jesus had paid. His target was to create envy, jealousy and hatred that would cause confusion and commotion in relationships. He is out as a roaring lion to rob humanity's precious future, stop joy, destroy life, attack our peace of mind, corrupt us with evil thoughts and create strongholds in our lives. Satan and his well-structured army of demons operate in stealth mode to cause confusion and destroy marriages, children, relationships, reputations, dreams and zeal of serving God. He is the archenemy of God and humanity, causing nations to rise against nations, but he is limited in power and time.

Our Lord Jesus unveiled the invisible war and the diabolic activities of this wicked one for us to understand that Satan's mission on earth is to cause confusion and war. "The thief cometh not, but for to steal, and to kill, and to destroy: I am come that they might have life, and that they might have it more abundantly" (John 10:10). As he didn't want to be subject to the authority of God on earth, his objective is to be worshipped (Luke 4:7-8). Worst still, he continues to entice the son of men with the lust of the flesh, lust of eyes and pride of life (1 John 2:15-17). This nature would be a gateway to satanic invasion, manipulation, oppression and hardness of heart against God.

Mysterious battles in the lives of so many Christians today are caused by Satan with a calculated attempt to keep man in perpetual bondage and rebellion like him. Believe it or not, spiritual warfare is a reality in this life. There is an invisible war being waged against every man and woman. With diverse problems and attacks, the devil moves against the family and marriage causing separation and divorce. The devil instigates commotion in the community and strategizes against the church to make her lukewarm, carnal, sensual and worldly. He's out there prowling with his evil intentions. As our spiritual adversary, he is always setting traps and causing his attacks in our thoughts and emotions. He's operates against leaders in the spiritual and secular. Satan opposes pastors and every believer who have given their lives to Jesus Christ as their Lord and Saviour by tempting them to do contrary to God's will and purpose.

Satan, the archenemy of humanity, the prince of that dark, invisible kingdom, orders thousands of wily and powerful demons on assignment to carry out evil onslaughts and wreak havocs in every area of one's life. He is also bent on overthrowing the Christian's faith with fear in order to defeat God's people and hinder the blessings of God in the life of His people. But the good news is that Satan has been defeated, and Christ has delegated His authority over Satan and his demonic forces to all believers who follow Him day by day. "And he said unto them, I beheld Satan as lightning fall from heaven. Behold, I give unto you power to tread on serpents and scorpions, and over all the power of the enemy: and nothing shall by any means hurt you" (Luke 10:18-19).

With this authority, we exercise dominion over Satan and his cohorts and this authority is only for every child of God today. Are you a child of God? Have you repented of your sins and renounced them? Have you given your life to Jesus by accepting Him as your Lord and Saviour? Please, do so if you have not. Faith in Christ will translate any sinner that comes to Him with a penitent heart from the kingdom of darkness into the Kingdom of light. And victory shall be your portion in Jesus' mighty name! "Giving thanks unto the Father, which hath made us meet to be partakers of the inheritance of the saints in light: Who hath delivered us from the power of darkness, and hath translated us into the kingdom of his dear Son" (Colossians 1:11-13).

Spiritual eagles will always engage the enemy from a high altitude of faith in God with all spiritual armours to win. We, as Christians, are sitting in heavenly paces with Christ and with all divine provisions of God's backing to defeat this old-time enemy of humanity and win in every battle that's trying to attend our ways.

OPERATIONS AND MANIFESTATIONS OF DEMONS

"Now the Spirit speaketh expressly, that in the latter times some shall depart from the faith, giving heed to seducing spirits, and doctrines of devils… Then was brought unto him one possessed with a devil, blind, and dumb: and he healed him, insomuch that the blind and dumb both spake and saw… And when they had gone through the isle unto Paphos, they found a certain sorcerer, a false prophet, a Jew, whose name was Barjesus: Which was with the deputy of the country, Sergius Paulus, a prudent man; who called for Barnabas and Saul, and desired to hear the word of God. But Elymas the sorcerer (for so is his name by interpretation) withstood them, seeking to turn away the deputy from the faith" (1 Timothy 4:1; Matthew 12:22; Acts 13:1-8).

Demons are very strategic to Satan's operations and activities in the world. Being not omnipresent, Satan accomplishes his purpose for nations, cities and whole communities through their instrumentality (Daniel 10:13; Revelation 16:13-14). Satan works through his demons to manipulate, intimidate, possess and consequently, dominate his victims. Demons are wicked in operations, their subtle activities are to entice people to do evil, captivate the mind and body and through deception, lead souls into falsehood and addiction of sinful practices that could lead to total destruction.

They are also responsible for many cases of bodily afflictions, mental derangement and torture. These activities can be broadly grouped into three, namely: oppression, obsession and possession. These were fully described in one of my books (Satanic attacks and the way out). The personality of a demon is often revealed in the behavioural pattern of its victim. For instance, demons are often referred to as unclean spirits and they promote gross uncleanness in and through their victims. We must, however, be careful lest we fall into the error of explaining away the corruption of the depraved nature with the activities of demons. Most demon-related problems are self-inflicted.

In other words, demonic inroads are created into people's lives through their carelessness and curiosity. Such inroads include participation in idolatrous rites, consulting witch-doctors/herbalists and immoral involvement with demon-infested personalities like prostitutes. Deliberate and prolonged listening to Satan-inspired music, demonic games/toys can also lead to demonic invasion. Some other people are demonized through pride-promoting organizations and social clubs (Ecclesiastes 10:8; Leviticus 19:31; John 13:27).

Nevertheless, Christ has both the power and willingness to deliver all who are oppressed of the devil and all those miraculous deliverance in the Scriptures prove the fact that He has power to solve all human problems (Acts 10:38). However, there is need for the victims to meet Christ's terms for full deliverance and healing. God demands full repentance from all sins, restitution where necessary and renunciation of all evil associations. Thereafter, he can approach the throne of grace to appropriate the provisions of Calvary for his deliverance as stated, "if the Son therefore shall make you free, ye shall be free indeed" (John 3:16; 8:36). Evidently, the miraculous signs and wonders of Jesus in His earthly ministry recorded in the Bible confirm and testify to the truth that Jesus is indeed the Saviour, Redeemer, Christ and the Son of the Highest God.

These are enough indisputable evidences for anyone on the surface of earth to believe in Jesus Christ as Lord and Saviour from the impending danger of everlasting punishment awaiting all the followers of Satan; and through believing, they receive everlasting life in His name (John 20:31).

Chapter 2

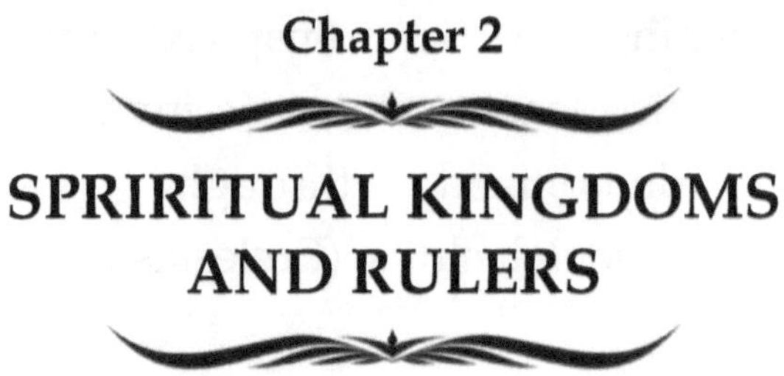

SPRIRITUAL KINGDOMS AND RULERS

"Again, the devil taketh him up into an exceeding high mountain, and sheweth him all the kingdoms of the world, and the glory of them; And saith unto him, All these things will I give thee, if thou wilt fall down and worship me … Giving thanks unto the Father, which hath made us meet to be partakers of the inheritance of the saints in light: Who hath delivered us from the power of darkness, and hath translated us into the kingdom of his dear Son: In whom we have redemption through his blood, even the forgiveness of sins: Who is the image of the invisible God, the firstborn of every creature" (Matthew 4:8-9; Colossians 1:12-15).

The Bible references above confirmed the two kingdoms (the kingdom of God and that of Satan). Satan always imitates and counterfeits all things that are of God. He also uses everything in his kingdom, which is just for a short time, to engage Christians is war continually. This enemy of our souls launches deadly attacks against believers in order to depopulate God's kingdom because he knows that he has a limited time and that the kingdoms of this world are becoming the Kingdom of our Lord Jesus Christ. "And the seventh angel sounded; and there were great voices in heaven, saying, the kingdoms of this world are become the kingdoms of our Lord, and of his Christ; and he shall reign for ever and ever" (Revelation 11:15).

There is a natural world that is visibly and we (humans) partly belong to it for a while. In other words, it is a global village comprised of continents, countries, provinces/states, cities and tribes. These are physical or natural kingdoms of people who are governed by chiefs, kings, emperors, governors, presidents and prime ministers. Also, there is a spiritual world which consists of the Kingdom of God and the (temporary) kingdom of Satan.

God is the Creator and Owner of the Kingdom of Heaven and earth, but Satan is being mischievous by using his deceptive acts to gain control of the minds of men on the surface of earth. "But God giveth it a body as it hath pleased him, and to every seed his own body. All flesh is not the same flesh: but there is one kind of flesh of men, another flesh of beasts, another of fishes, and another of birds. There are also celestial bodies, and bodies terrestrial: but the glory of the celestial is one, and the glory of the terrestrial is another" (1 Corinthians 15:38-40).

Of course, NASA spies and ufologists said they sighted Extra-Terrestrials (ETs) who are said to have been navigating the earth on flying saucers and spaceships. Some call them Unidentified Flying Objects (UFOs) because they cannot be identified or explained and are often associated with aliens and conspiracy theories.

God's Kingdom is ruled by God the Father, His Son Jesus Christ and the Holy Spirit. The citizens of this Kingdom are the saints and other occupants are the holy angels who minister to the needs of the saints of God. "For there are three that bear record in heaven, the Father, the Word, and the Holy Ghost: and these three are one…And the angel said unto them, Fear not: for, behold, I bring you good tidings of great joy, which shall be to all people" (1 John 5:7; Luke 2:10).

On the contrary, Satan's kingdom comprises of Satan himself, demons and sinners who refused to give their lives to Jesus Christ. These ones will end up with Satan in the Lake of Fire. The overall aim of Satan and his demons is to attack their victims, demonize them, torment them and control their minds.

Believe it or not, both believers and unbelievers are continually engaged in every battle of life orchestrated by the enemy of our souls and there's no neutral ground as no one is immune from this battle caused by Satan. The invisible battle takes place in the realm of the spirit continually because Satan wants to enslave the souls of men in sins and rebellion against God incessantly in order to ensure that they eventually end up in the Lake of Fire prepared for him and his cohorts. (Matthew 25:41).

The early church was fully aware of this fact and was engaged in an intense spiritual battle against satanic threats, attacks, oppressions and wickedness. This is the reason Paul the apostle declared that, "For we wrestle not against flesh and blood, but against principalities, against powers, against the rulers of the darkness of this world, against spiritual wickedness in high places" (Ephesians 6:12). Worst still, many people are ignorant of the devices Satan and his demons.

THE ORIGIN OF ANGELS

"For by him were all things created, that are in heaven, and that are in earth, visible and invisible, whether they be thrones, or dominions, or principalities, or powers: all things were created by him, and for him…Are they not all ministering spirits, sent forth to minister for them who shall be heirs of salvation?" (Colossians 1:16; Hebrews 1:14).

Angels are spiritual living creatures created by God. They did not evolve from some blind chance. They were created to both glorify and worship God and the Lord Jesus Christ (Hebrews 1:6). Far inferior to God the Father, Son and the Holy Spirit, they are the ministering spirits assigned to minister to the need of saints and to do God's perfect will. They are holy (Matthew 25:31) and tasked to worship and serve the Almighty God. They are many and classified according to the duties they need to perform with special functions. As messengers of God, they are to carry out God's will in heaven and earth such as to warn, sustain, deliver, protect, provide guidance and help God's people. They are:

Cherubims – They are the highest order of God's angels, the living creatures that surround God's throne. They are designated to protect the Garden of Eden. (Genesis 3:24; Exodus 25:18-22; Revelation 4:6).

Seraphims – They are the ministers that lead the heavenly worship of God and proclaim the supremacy of the glory of His holiness. They also serve as agents of purification in order to fulfil God's purpose. (Isaiah 6:2, 6).

Also, there are **Elect angels** according to 1 Timothy 5:21, "I charge thee before God, and the Lord Jesus Christ, and the elect angels, that thou observe these things without preferring one before another, doing nothing by partiality."

Michael – An archangel in charge of the army angels of God. (Daniel 10:13, 21; Jude 9; Revelation 12:7).

Gabriel – An angel assigned to deliver important messages from God to His people. (Luke 1:19, 26; Daniel 8:16; 9:21).

In general, angels are immortal (Luke 20:34-36); intelligent (2 Samuel 14:20); have visible and invisible forms (Numbers 22:22-25); they are obedient to God (Psalms 103:20); innumerable (Psalms 68:17; Luke 2:13; Hebrews 12:12); powerful (Psalms 103:20; 2 Peter 2:11); sexless and do not marry (Luke 20:34-36); they are holy (Revelation 14:10); their duty and activities are to worship God (Matthew 18:10). The source of their power is both given and governed by God. They are active in both heaven and earth (universally) with privilege to have access to God's presence in Heaven.

The future roles of Godly angels include:
- Accompanying our Lord Jesus Christ in His return to rapture the saints – 1 Thessalonians 4:16.
- Assembling of God's elects in the final harvest of the world – Matthew 24:31.

- Involving in preaching during the Great Tribulation – Revelation 14:6-9.
- Separating the righteous from the wicked – Matthew 13:39.
- Binding Satan for a thousand years – Revelation 20:1-2.

God, in His infinite power, has created all things for His pleasure including the invisible world such as principalities and power, thrones, dominions and the Milky Way. The angels' assignment ranges from one position to the other. There are ruling angels – Principalities, powers, thrones, authorities, dominions and might. In the same vein, Satan has a counterfeit kingdom, thrones and power of evil forces. "For by him were all things created, that are in heaven, and that are in earth, visible and invisible, whether they be thrones, or dominions, or principalities, or powers: all things were created by him, and for him… To the intent that now unto the principalities and powers in heavenly places might be known by the church the manifold wisdom of God" (Colossians 1:16; Ephesians 3:10).

Angels were originally created without sin like Adam until the chief angel - Lucifer instigated a plot to overthrow the Almighty God. He succeeded in convincing one-third of the angels in Heaven along with him to carry out his evil plan. Since they couldn't win and would never have won, however, they were cast down along with Satan - the master they chose to follow (Revelation 12:3-4, 9).

SATAN – THE CHIEF RULER OF DARKNESS

Jesus Christ is both the Prince of Life and Peace (Acts 3:15; Isaiah 9:6) and Jesus called Satan the prince this world (John 14:30) and also the prince of air, the chief ruler of darkness (Ephesians 2:2). In Hebrew, the word 'Satan' means the adversary, the commander of the armies of darkness, accuser and enemy of both human and celestial beings alike. He is the devil (*diabolos* in Greek), the slanderer, the ruler of this world (John 8:44), god of this world (2 Corinthians 4:4), father of lies (John 8:44), ruler of the power of the air (Ephesians 2:2), and Beelzebub, the prince of the devils (Mark 3:22) and the chief of the devils or ruler of demons (Luke 11:15).

Satan is the prince of the power of the air that rules over demons and the world system. The power of the air refers to satanic strongholds, the hosts of demons and spiritual forces of wickedness in heavenly places. "Wherein in time past ye walked according to the course of this world, according to the prince of the power of the air, the spirit that now worketh in the children of disobedience: Among whom also we all had our conversation in times past in the lusts of our flesh, fulfilling the desires of the flesh and of the mind; and were by nature the children of wrath, even as others" (Ephesians 2:2-3).

Satan's kingdom is characterized by the bondage of sin, rebellion and the curses brought upon humanity for disobedience and unrighteous living. It is the spirit that controls, directs and orders every person that is not saved.

They walk in the flesh and not in the Spirit of God. They are rebellious and subject to the dictates of satanic rules, regulations and influence. All the wisdom of wickedness, oppression, unbelief, rebellion, witch-crafts and evils emanates from the realm of the operations of the power of air, the sphere of invisible belt around the world. As a prince, Satan has a demonic kingdom (Matthew 12:26); and a throne (Revelation 2:13) and as a ruler, he possesses power to manipulate and manifest evil in the entire world through his demons and human agents.

With all his deception and authority over the world system, his power is limited, his kingdom is divided and his time of government is temporary on earth, as the Bible confirmed. "And the seventh angel sounded; and there were great voices in heaven, saying, the kingdoms of this world are become the kingdoms of our Lord, and of his Christ; and he shall reign for ever and ever" (Revelation 11:15).

Both heaven and earth are under the overall control of the Sovereign God, whose Kingdom is from everlasting to everlasting (Romans 16:20; Psalms 145:13). However, Jesus Himself called Satan the prince of this world. This means that our Lord Jesus knows the activities of this accuser of the brethren and knows the best opportune time the devil entices and tempts us to sin. Jesus said, "…for the prince of this world cometh, and hath nothing in me" (John 14:30). This calls for watchfulness on the part of all believers with self-examination, perseverance and prayers. Nothing must entice us in this world to sin against God.

PRINCIPALITIES AND POWERS

Principalities and powers are among the fallen angels with greater levels of authority than demons (Ephesians 3:10). According to Consolidated Webster Encyclopedic Dictionary, 'principality' means sovereignty; supreme power, a prince; one invested with sovereignty; the territory of a prince. A principality (could be a General in rank) is a seat of authority in the whole spiritual realm where spiritual entities of invisible angels, demons and princes dwell.

Power could be a lower rank officer assigned to kill or destroy.

In general, Satan, the prince of the power of the air, is the archenemy of God and mankind. He controls the forces of the cosmos, traditions, world orders and lifestyles. He has designated princes with power and authority to rule over their empires, territories, provinces, states and countries. This prince rules over the principality in his empire, nation or state and holds their power within their jurisdiction with influence and authority. These ruling demonic spirits possess the people in government and authorities in organizations of every nation and territory to do contrary to God's will and purpose on earth.

In Matthew 12:24, Beelzebub is called the prince of demons that operates under Satan's dominion. It is the wicked spirit that rules, controls and directs the world's system and many organizations today. Also, the activities of these principalities and power are what Daniel experienced in his day. "But the prince of the kingdom of Persia withstood me one and twenty days: but, lo, Michael, one of the chief princes, came to help me; and I remained there with the kings of Persia" (Daniel 10:13).

Nevertheless, the ultimate power and authority belong to God, Who will judge all things including these principalities and power that derived pleasure in using their limited power to oppress and intimidate because they (both Satan and his cohorts) have a limited time. "And it shall come to pass in that day, that the LORD shall punish the host of the high ones that are on high, and the kings of the earth upon the earth" (Isaiah 24:21). But for those who have given their lives to Jesus Christ as their Lord and Saviour, He (Jesus) is their Prince. He is the Prince of peace, the Lord of lords, the incoming King whose Kingdom has no end (Isaiah 9:6-7; Revelation 19:16).

The knowledge of this truth will instruct, enable and encourage Christian pilgrims in the battle field of life to put their trust in God in all spiritual warfare as the battle is the Lords. Are you on the Lord's side? Who is your prince? Jesus or Satan? Remember that you can't seat on the fence. It is either you belong to the camp of the Prince of peace (Jesus) whose government has no end or to that of the prince of the power of the air (Satan) with limited power and time.

RULERS OF DARKNESS

"And you hath he quickened, who were dead in trespasses and sins; Wherein in time past ye walked according to the course of this world, according to the prince of the power of the air, the spirit that now worketh in the children of disobedience: Among whom also we all had our conversation in times past in the lusts of our flesh, fulfilling the desires of the flesh and of the mind; and were by nature the children of wrath, even as others" (Ephesians 2:1-3).

The beautiful thing to know is that believers have Jesus Christ as their Prince of peace that rules their hearts in situations. There is nothing these believers have to fear about the ruler of darkness because they live in intimate relationship with Christ and at close proximity to His Kingdom contact and postal address. But Satan, his demons, all the natures and lifestyles outside God's Kingdom are being controlled by the rulers of darkness with Satan that lives in darkness as their head.

People in darkness hate the truth and oppose the light of God that is supposed to shine upon them to have eternal life. Darkness is associated with Satan's power and death. Through human ignorance, Satan has succeeded in his wiles of accusation, harassment, deception and temptation to blindfold, cripple and steal people's peace, joy, marriage, progress and health; he drains them up until life is sniffed out of them and distracts them from God's plan of salvation. The lust of the eyes and the lust of our flesh involve fulfilling the sinful desires of the flesh and of the mind that are the nature of the children of wrath being controlled by the rulers of darkness and demons.

SPIRITUAL WICKEDNESS IN HIGH PLACES

Spiritual wickedness in high places exists in the lower heaven of stars and cloud. This is the location of invisible meeting places of wicked forces of dark powers that backs up witchcraft activities, apostate monsters and the occult world in the second heaven. Evil forces get directives from the rulers of darkness to perpetrate evil onslaught in human's life. They are the demonic forces causing all problems in the lives of people and churches to hinder the salvation of souls, estop revival and limit the expansion of God's Kingdom on earth.

Furthermore, the activities of spiritual wickedness in high places are to cause series of incurable sicknesses, epidemics and pandemic diseases such as the novel or new Coronavirus (nCOVID-19) ravaging the world since late 2019. They cause afflictions, nightmares and untold hardships and also place heavy yokes upon innocent victims or those who offend them. They manipulate their lives, cage their destiny, block their opportunities, seize their blessings, cause mysterious accidents and bring untimely death to them.

The operation of spiritual wickedness in high places are not far from individuals that harbour animosity, hatred and unforgiveness with murderous spirit to kill their fellow human beings at all costs. Defilement and perverting judgement by allowing evil to thrive with impunity is nothing but spiritual wickedness.

In other words, the act of wickedness is Satan's nature and it is normal in his kingdom. Spiritual wickedness manifests in the works of the flesh that Paul enumerated in Galatians 5:19-21, "Now the works of the flesh are manifest, which are these; Adultery, fornication, uncleanness, lasciviousness, Idolatry, witchcraft, hatred, variance, emulations, wrath, strife, seditions, heresies, Envyings, murders, drunkenness, revellings, and such like: of the which I tell you before, as I have also told you in time past, that they which do such things shall not inherit the kingdom of God."

THE PRINCE OF PERSIA

"When a strong man armed keepeth his palace, his goods are in peace: But when a stronger than he shall come upon him, and overcome him, he taketh from him all his armour wherein he trusted, and divideth his spoils" (Luke 11:21-22). Satan cannot be overestimated because he has been defeated by Christ. At the same time, he cannot be underestimated because he is full of subtlety to take advantage of this truth. Believers must be careful and understand how the devil entices, deceives and manipulates things to have his way. He is not omnipresent in nature but he has his emissaries in every geographical location, territory and nation, who voluntarily succumb to his dictates. A typical example is the prince of Persia (a strongman assigned to fulfill the purpose of Satan in that territory).

"In the third year of Cyrus king of Persia a thing was revealed unto Daniel, whose name was called Belteshazzar; and the thing was true, but the time appointed was long:

and he understood the thing, and had understanding of the vision. In those days I Daniel was mourning three full weeks. I ate no pleasant bread, neither came flesh nor wine in my mouth, neither did I anoint myself at all, till three whole weeks were fulfilled…Then said he unto me, Fear not, Daniel: for from the first day that thou didst set thine heart to understand, and to chasten thyself before thy God, thy words were heard, and I am come for thy words. But the prince of the kingdom of Persia withstood me one and twenty days: but, lo, Michael, one of the chief princes, came to help me; and I remained there with the kings of Persia" (Daniel 10:1-3, 12-13).

This is the strongman between Daniel and his answer to prayers. The problem in Daniel's life is not only physical but spiritual because God had to intervene by sending Archangel Michael for his rescue. Sometimes, the strongman in the territory, state or area may be the controlling invisible power standing between you and your divine destiny. The strongman is assigned to steal from you, block and lock your prayers; and cause mysterious sicknesses, poverty and premature death in many cases. The devil, in his craftiness, will always act as a roaring lion but he has been defeated by the true Lion of the tribe of Judah; hence the need for understanding (1 John 3:8; Proverbs 4:7).

In some territories, the strongman hinders the propagation of the gospel of Christ, the fellowship of believers and prayers of the brethren (Daniel 6:12; Romans 8:35; Galatians 1:13). The essence of these demonic strongholds and strongmen in geographical locations of continents and nations were as a result of evil consecrations and dedications, covenants with idols, coupled with all forms of rituals, shedding of innocent blood at the base of spiritual foundation and demonic strongholds in the territorial regions of the surface of the whole earth. "That innocent blood be not shed in thy land, which the Lord thy God giveth thee for an inheritance, and so blood be upon thee" (Deuteronomy 19:10). These demonic strongholds, fortresses or strong rooms are in the air, land and water to hinder progress, weaken saints' spiritual power, hold down blessings and prosperity, attack relationships, break families, prevent stability and disturb peace.

The only language the devil understands is war! He won't leave your territory with ease unless you declare a total war armed with God's weapons of warfare at your disposal to unseat him and his emissaries. The Bible says, "Resist the devil and he will flee from you" (1 Peter 5:8-9).

The Christian life is full of battles and spiritual warfare. Hence Christians that would like to make spiritual progress won't stand aloof because, "we wrestle not against flesh and blood… (Amos 6:1; Ephesians 6:12). The devil will never release all that he has taken from us on a silver platter. Only the violent can take it by force from him (Matthew 18:18-19). This means, believers need to be strong in the Lord and in the power of His might in order to confront the devil and his wicked acts with the power of the Holy Ghost to set the captive free. Only those who know their God shall be strong and do exploits in His Kingdom (Daniel 11:32).

The good Lord is looking for those who would allow God to use them for others, by standing in the gap to pull down Satan's strongholds of bondages, destroy evil altars and communication networks, chains, shackles, yokes; and then subdue and spoil the devil's kingdom for souls of men to be saved. All captives of the mighty must be set free; those that have been subject to the fear of death all their lifetime must be delivered; as many as are chained with heavy yokes and bondage of the strongman must be liberated and those laden with sicknesses, oppressions and infirmities need to be healed and set at liberty in Christ. "For though we walk in the flesh, we do not war according to the flesh. For the weapons of our warfare are not carnal but mighty in God for pulling down strongholds, casting down arguments and every high thing that exalts itself against the knowledge of God, bringing every thought into captivity to the obedience of Christ, and being ready to punish all disobedience when your obedience is fulfilled" (2 Corinthians 10:3-6).

Through our obedience to the Captain of our salvation, perseverance of faith, boldness and courage, believers can deal a deathblow to every strongman that is militating against them in every area of life. There is nothing to fear because Satan and his cohorts have been defeated by Christ since more than two millennia ago. With Christ's delegated power and authority given to us (Luke 10:17-19; Matthew 4:23-24), we need to put this archenemy where he belongs -

under our feet (Romans 16:20). The armed strongman, whose palace is well-guarded and his stolen goods are secure, must be spoiled as Christ did. Jesus destroyed the works of the devil by casting out demons from the people and liberating them from the hold of Satan up until today. He demonstrated it and has also given us the power to do likewise as we go out to preach the gospel to every creature.

MARINE KINGDOM OF DARKNESS

"Get thee unto Pharaoh in the morning; lo, he goeth out unto the water; and thou shalt stand by the river's brink against he come; and the rod which was turned to a serpent shalt thou take in thine hand...Speak, and say, Thus saith the Lord God; Behold, I am against thee, Pharaoh king of Egypt, the great dragon that lieth in the midst of his rivers, which hath said, My river is mine own, and I have made it for myself" (Exodus 7:15; Ezekiel 29:3).

Pharaoh represents a principality that draws his strength from the water spirits of his stronghold. They are known as aquatic spirits of the marine kingdom. There are spiritual realms in the universe which are the heavenlies, the earth and the waters. Water is one of the strongholds that the devil has built and fortified for his evil activities after the second heaven and earth. The marine kingdom represents the water spirits that dwell in oceans, seas, rivers, lakes, streams and brooks with attendant occultic practices of witchcraft, rituals and other diabolic activities. "Dead things are formed from under the waters, and the inhabitants thereof" (Job 26:5).

Marine kingdom is Satan's realm of evil activities where power and position seekers, wealth seekers, fetish priests and water worshippers visit regularly to carry out their demonic activities that affect the natural world. Also, there are marine witchcraft covens under the water where people's spirits are invoked, evil decisions get made and wicked judgements are pronounced on them to destroy their lives. Many issues are being settled spiritually in this realm before we see their physical manifestation in form of series of attacks and mysterious occurrences in the lives of men.

Imagine if the devil had no regards to attack our Lord Jesus by causing an intense sea storm or cyclone when He and his disciples were crossing the sea of Galilee (Mark 5), Christians need to put on the whole armour of God and prepare for war at all times by watching and praying without ceasing. The entire coastland region of Gadara had been held captive for a very long time by Satan. However, he tried to hinder the people' salvation and deliverance knowing full well that Jesus and His disciples would be a threat to his demonic activities in the whole countryside.

During my Secondary days in my country of birth, there was a boy whose name originated from the river because of the ancestral worship of marine deities. The family members worship aquatic demons or water spirit and were dedicated to them. Through the priest, they requested a male child from the river deity when one of the family members was barren. This boy was extremely stubborn and had no respect for anyone, not even for the school authority. He normally went to this river to swim but always violated the rules given by the goddess by doing abominable things in the river. The rebellious attitude of this boy always provoked and caused the mermaid of this river to come out in broad daylight with annoyance to issue serious warnings to this boy, yet, he never listened but continued as usual.

Worst still, the boy told his friends in the school about his encounter with the mermaid, he requested that his friends, ten of them, should accompany him to swim during the school break period (11:00 a.m.). Eleven of them left the school unnoticed to swim.

As usual, he committed abominable things that would force the mermaid to come out as usual. But this time, the river goddess refused to come out as he had narrated to his friends. Therefore, in order to further provoke the mermaid, the boy jumped into the river. For a while, his friends didn't see any sign of him but what they began to hear from this boy as he cried out was, 'Please rescue me! rescue me!! rescue me!!!' in the local language. His cry attracted the sympathy of other friends and they also decided to jump into the river with the aim of rescuing him.

Unfortunately, it was contrary to what they expected, the river washed them away. The expert swimmers that were watching afar off jumped into the river and were able to rescue the ten friends without this boy. The incident was reported to the parents of the boy and since the family priest of the river came from this family, they returned to the river to search for their boy up until 10:00 p.m. This worried the entire family members that were worshipping this river. The following day, they found the boy dead at the brink of the river. His two eyes had been eaten along with his private part, one hand and one leg. According to the tradition, any person that got killed that way must be buried at the river bank. Therefore, the family consulted the river goddess on what caused the death of this boy.

The mermaid came out and fully explained the degree of humiliation she has suffered as a result of the stubbornness of the boy who refused to keep to the covenants that govern their relationship. According to the eyewitness in the family, the mermaid's intention was not to kill him but to punish him for some days in order for him to learn. However, her children have started eating him before she returned from the market because they thought that the boy was a meal for them. All efforts to resuscitate him failed and he died. Stubbornness is the very nature of Satan. He can't give a free gift without a dare consequence attached to it and all the reign of terror of the wicked one in this world is for a very short time.

Nevertheless, "Thus saith the Lord God to Tyrus; Shall not the isles shake at the sound of thy fall, when the wounded cry, when the slaughter is made in the midst of thee? Then all the princes of the sea shall come down from their thrones, and lay away their robes, and put off their broidered garments: they shall clothe themselves with trembling; they shall sit upon the ground, and shall tremble at every moment, and be astonished at thee. And they shall take up a lamentation for thee, and say to thee, How art thou destroyed, that wast inhabited of seafaring men, the renowned city, which wast strong in the sea, she and her inhabitants, which cause their terror to be on all that haunt it! Now shall the isles tremble in the day of thy fall; yea, the isles that are in the sea shall be troubled at thy departure" (Ezekiel 26:15-18).

Another friend of mine who is a Christian leader was being afflicted for many years. As the only born-again Christian in the family, he noticed that his siblings were not having the experience of severe attacks that he suffered. Therefore, he decided to visit his mother to enquire about the circumstances surrounding his situation. His mother confessed to him that she had a covenant with the water-goddess and requested all her children from the water spirit. She explained further that, any of her children that breaks the covenant with this goddess shall have afflictions. "As the bird by wandering, as the swallow by flying, so the curse causeless shall not come" (Proverbs 26:2).

The confession of the old woman opened the eyes of my friend to engage in spiritual warfare for total freedom. Of course, his case was different because he is born again! Jesus said, "If the world hate you, ye know that it hated me before it hated you. If ye were of the world, the world would love his own: but because ye are not of the world, but I have chosen you out of the world, therefore the world hateth you." (John 15:18-19). Apostle John also said, "Marvel not, my brethren, if the world hate you." (1 John 3:13)

Unfortunately, some Christians are still suffering from the foundational issues of family background. The generational tides and curses that come from breaking covenant with the family must be broken completely. It is extremely dangerous for Christian to fall in love with a person possessed with water spirit because marine agents bring terrible oppression, afflictions and untold hardships on their captives. But "In that day the LORD with his sore and great and strong sword shall punish leviathan the piercing serpent, even leviathan that crooked serpent; and he shall slay the dragon that is in the sea" (Isaiah 27:1).

The serpentine spirit of the marine kingdom is the source of witchcraft and divination. The Almighty God has to declare His decision to punish this monster because it is the stubborn spirit that has the power to manipulate, seduce, attack and possess a person that has relationship with it. It is the source of many financial failures and deaths today through curses, spells, voodoo and incantations. It promotes rebellion, divination, and witchcraft.

These evil activities take place in the marine world to crush and destroy the vision, dreams and hope of the Church and disrupt people's life on the earth. Except there's genuine repentance and salvation in Christ Jesus with prayers, those who are under the captivity of the marine kingdom of darkness struggle in life to fulfil destiny. The demon of a python or serpentine spirit from the marine world can enter a person through family dedication to a deity such as a river god or goddess. Evil patterns arising from river worship eventually subject the captive to series of bewitchment, immorality and other oppressive experiences.

Chapter 3

OCCULT SATANIC WORSHIP

"And have no fellowship with the unfruitful works of darkness, but rather reprove them. For it is a shame even to speak of those things which are done of them in secret. ... I will also stretch out mine hand upon Judah, and upon all the inhabitants of Jerusalem; and I will cut off the remnant of Baal from this place, and the name of the Chemarims with the priests; And them that worship the host of heaven upon the housetops; and them that worship and that swear by the Lord, and that swear by Malcham" (Ephesians 5:11-12; Zephaniah 1:4-5).

Occult is the hidden work of darkness carried out to acquire personal power for self-gratification. The people involved in occult interact with the spirit world that is not acquainted with Jesus Christ, the Son of the living God. Thus, occultic practices promote the propagation of the doctrine of Satan and his evil forces. Examples are White magic, Divination, Clairvoyance, Idolatry, Wicca, Neo-paganism, Voodoo, Seances, Telepathy, Necromancy, Kabbalah Mysticism, Esoterism, Sorcery, Exorcism, Freemasonry, Illuminati, Spiritualism, Eckankar, Rosicrucianism, Theosophy, Astronomy, Zodiacs, Astrology/Astral projection, Fortune telling, Prognostication, Prestidigitation, Metaphysics, Psychics, Transcendental meditation, Numerology, Witchcraft, Wizardry, Familiar Spiritism, Yoga, Mediumism/

Mediumship, the use Ouija boards, Crystal balls and Satanism, which are all abominations unto the Lord.

"You shall have no other gods before Me. You shall not make for yourself a carved image — any likeness of anything that is in heaven above, or that is in the earth beneath, or that is in the water under the earth; you shall not bow down to them nor serve them. For I, the Lord your God, am a jealous God, visiting the iniquity of the fathers upon the children to the third and fourth generations of those who hate Me" (Exodus 20:3-5). These practices have enslaved many people and bound them up in the diabolical web of demonic influences through the worship of Satan. Unfortunately, some so-called pastors and ministers didn't see any of these practices as evil. They put one leg in the church and other leg in occultism.

The testimony of a woman that got converted from satanism exposed some preachers of the gospel that engaged in this act. She said that some pastors initiated their church members through the Lord's Supper, feast foods and the use of anointing oil. Some are also demonized through the laying on of hands of such leaders with occultic rings on their fingers. As a result, many church members are suffering today from demonic harassment that could come through nightmares, mysterious sicknesses, attacks, usual fears and torments of the devil. For those who were directly involved in occultic practices, these activities give the devil a foothold and legal right to attack and enslave them.

However, such leaders that are engaged in any of these evil practices will have a case to answer in the Court of Heaven!

DIVINATION

Divination is an illegitimate means of determining God's will through the inspiration of Satan or evil spirits. "There shall not be found among you anyone who makes his son or his daughter pass through the fire, or one who practices witchcraft, or a soothsayer, or one who interprets omens, or a sorcerer, or one who conjures spells, or a medium, or a spiritist, or one who calls up the dead. For all who do these things are an abomination to the LORD, and because of these abominations the LORD your God drives them out from before you" (Deuteronomy 18:10-12).

The spirit of divination is the spirit of Satan that uncovers hidden knowledge by supernatural means. This practice sometimes includes the killing of some animals to observe its liver in order to get direction or guidance for the future. "For the king of Babylon stands at the parting of the road, at the fork of the two roads, to use divination: he shakes the arrows, he consults the images, he looks at the liver" (Ezekiel 21:21 NKJV).

Some Christians are still practicing the ministry of king Saul who could not hear from God because of rebellion and sin. Instead of seeking God's face for genuine repentance and restoration, he proceeds further to seek for personal prophecy through the spirit of divination (1 Samuel 28:6-7). The spirit of divination is used by false prophets, diviners, consulters of familiar spirits, enchanters, sorcerers, soothsayers, necromancers, wizards, witches and astrologers.

Those who are involved in these practices are working contrary to God's express command and are invoking the wrath of God upon themselves except they repent before it is too late. "And the soul that turneth after such as have familiar spirits, and after wizards, to go a whoring after them, I will even set my face against that soul, and will cut him off from among his people. Sanctify yourselves therefore, and be ye holy: for I am the LORD your God" (Leviticus 20:6-7). The true prophets of God in Bible days spoke God's mind to the people for edification, encouragement, counselling and warning believers of any impending danger. They also rebuke sin in order bring the erring people back to God. But the false prophets, through the spirit of divination, will prophesy material things and bring false hope to the people.

NECROMANCY

Necromancy is an extension of divination by communicating with dead spirits. Some attest to the erroneous belief that a deceased ancestor is their god who guides the family in taking right decisions on their lives. As a result, libations or drinks offerings or sacrifice could be poured out to the deceased in adoration. This is contrary to God's Word. "And when they shall say unto you, seek unto them that have familiar spirits and unto wizards that peep, and that mutter: should not a people seek unto their God? for the living to the dead? To the law and to the testimony: if they speak not according to this word, it is because there is no light in them" (Isaiah 8:19-20).

Another way of practicing necromancy is seances, the agency of medium (channelling) to communicate with the dead through a group of people sitting in a circle, by holding their hands to summon a deceased person in order to acquire certain information that is not physically available to them. It is important to know that God is against necromancy and would never allow the medium of Endor to have access to Samuel's spirit who is resting in the bosom of the Lord. The Lord will not communicate with backslider (1 Samuel 28:6-20). The pseudo conjuration of the spirit of Samuel by the witch of Endor is nothing but a demonic manipulation, satanic deception, a parody and total counterfeit!

Psychic practice is another form of modern necromancy (the use of extrasensory perception to identify hidden information from the normal senses, involving telepathy or clairvoyance (Psychic Wikipedia). However, God frowns at whosoever makes a contact with the spirit of the devil. Such a person would bear the deserved consequences of violating God's warning (Isaiah 47:9-13).

MAGIC

"Then Pharaoh also called the wise men and the sorcerers: now the magicians of Egypt, they also did in like manner with their enchantments. For they cast down every man his rod, and they became serpents: but Aaron's rod swallowed up their rods" (Exodus 7:11-12). Magic is a technique of generating an expected outcome through the use of incantation, manipulation, or various demonic activities that is beyond human control. Magic supernaturally controls the forces of nature and may include the use of symbols, chants, rituals, gestures, actions and languages that contain unnatural power to conjure some result up for people to see.

In entertainment, it is used as acting illusion through deceptive devices of Satan to bring up results for audience to see. But from the Scriptural point of view, it is a process of mimicking the miracle God performed in the land of Egypt through Aaron and Moses. Therefore, magical power is from Satan with limited power of accomplishment but God's power is unlimited in the life of His anointed minister of the gospel. The evidence could be seen when Aaron's rod swallowed all the rods of the magicians in the land of Egypt (Exodus 7:9-12).

Whether it is white magic used to do good things or black magic to invoke evil through spells, curses or evil spirits to bring misfortunes upon someone, both sources of magical power are from Satan. Whatever your colour or race, if you are involved with magic or proud of this evil power, you are a candidate of hell if you refused to repent from this evil way and give your life to Jesus Christ.
"And many that believed came, and confessed, and shewed their deeds. Many of them also which used curious arts brought their books together, and burned them before all

men: and they counted the price of them, and found it fifty thousand pieces of silver. Then Peter opened his mouth, and said, of a truth I perceive that God is no respecter of persons: But in every nation he that feareth him, and worketh righteousness, is accepted with him" (Acts 19:18-19; 10:34-35).

The practical demonstration of genuine repentance is by open confession of all false ways and sinful acts, restitution and destruction of Satan's properties at our disposals. This means, we forsake all things for the excellency of the knowledge of the Lord Jesus Christ with absolute determination and trust to follow Him all the days of our lives. This way, we are telling Satan publicly that we have decamped from his kingdom into the everlasting Kingdom of Jesus Christ for the rest of our lives on earth. The decision is final and there is no turning back, come what may!

SORCERY

"But there was a certain man, called Simon, which before time in the same city used sorcery, and bewitched the people of Samaria, giving out that himself was some great one: To whom they all gave heed, from the least to the greatest, saying, This man is the great power of God. And to him they had regard, because that of long time he had bewitched them with sorceries" (Acts 8:9-11). Sorcery is closely connected to magic. It is the use of demonic power over the people by casting spells on them and it was totally forbidden by God. The sorcerer bypasses both the wisdom and power of God to foretell the future, control the environment and manipulate the people. This act gives glory the devil and it is an abomination unto the Lord. It carries severe punishment for those who engage in it (Malachi 3:5). It is a common practice in ancient Egypt and the kingdom of Babylon (Exodus 7:11; Daniel 2:2).

As a result, God warned the children of Israel to abstain from this evil the practice of sorcery. In this modern world, sorcery has been modernized and practiced freely with impunity everywhere - even in some churches! Some of the TV movies are fully saturated with sorcery activities. These End-times, there are many Elymas the sorcerers who preach on the pulpit today, bewitching and oppressing the people under them with diabolical power in order to put them in perpetual bondage due to their lifestyle of lying, misappropriation of church funds and sleeping with other members of the church secretly under the auspices of the so-called servant of God. If any member challenges their sinful acts, the so-called minister of God would intimidate them and cast spells and curses on them claiming that they will perish as Korah, Dothan and Abiram who spoke against Moses perished in one day.

Moses never used sorcery to bewitch the children of Israel, God's testimony concerning him was that he was the meekest man on earth in his own time (Numbers 12:3). When the children if Israel sinned, he interceded for them on several occasions, he also interceded for Korah, Dothan and Abirah before God's judgement fell on them. Inn some churches today, some people have been bewitched and couldn't challenge the evil that is going on in the church. Instead, they choose to remain silent in compromise.

Elymas the sorcerer knows how to attack the mind of the people under him to put them in perpetual bondage through bewitchment. As a liar, Elymas the sorcerer in the church would craftily cause division among brethren and create a big fight to cause members to leave the church. But "by their fruits, we shall know them." They have demonic anointing to cast spell on anyone who challenged their sinful acts, but they lack the power of the Holy Ghost and divine directive that could lead them to win more souls into the Kingdom of God.

ASTROLOGY

"Thou art wearied in the multitude of thy counsels. Let now the astrologers, the stargazers, the monthly prognosticators, stand up, and save thee from these things that shall come upon thee...Beware lest any man spoil you through philosophy and vain deceit, after the tradition of men, after the rudiments of the world, and not after Christ" (Isaiah 47:13; Colossians 2:8).

Astrology is the act of using the position of the stars, moon and the planets to predict the future and the attributes of people through twelve different zodiac signs. This is different from metaphysical prediction and astrological cult practiced in ancient Babylon. Canaan and Egypt worshipped stars and deities. This is idolatry, while Canaan astrology is centered on a bull, Baal worship and child sacrifice to Molech.

"Then God turned, and gave them up to worship the host of heaven; as it is written in the book of the prophets, O ye house of Israel, have ye offered to me slain beasts and sacrifices by the space of forty years in the wilderness? Yea, ye took up the tabernacle of Moloch, and the star of your god Remphan, figures which ye made to worship them: and I will carry you away beyond Babylon (Acts 7:42-43).

This indicates the worship of Saturn and stars. But Daniel was empowered with God-given wisdom and was ten times better than the wisdom of the astrologers and magicians in Babylon (Daniel 2:25-28). God's power is awesome, unlimited and ultimate.

HYPNOTISM

"And it came to pass, as we went to prayer, a certain damsel possessed with a spirit of divination met us, which brought her masters much gain by soothsaying: The same followed Paul and us, and cried, saying, These men are the servants of the most high God, which shew unto us the way of salvation. And this did she many days. But Paul, being grieved, turned and said to the spirit, I command thee in the name of Jesus Christ to come out of her. And he came out the same hour" (Acts 16:16-18). The damsel used the spirit of divination to bring gain to her masters. Using the power of Satan to bring gain either in our secular life or in God's service is the trick of the devil and an abomination unto the

Lord. For this purpose, Paul was grieved in spirit and cast out this spirit from the damsel.

Hypnotism is a form of enchantment, a meditative state to suppress the normal functioning of the brain. This technique is used in many cults and religions that could make one vulnerable to demonic manipulations and influences. Hypnotism has been used for many years by spirit medium, yogis, shamans, Buddhists, Hindus and witchdoctors. In this End-time, however, some professing Christians accept and practice hypnosis for treatment and some medical doctors, dentists, psychologists and psychiatrists are not left out.

EXTRASENSORY PERCEPTION (ESP) USED BY FALSE PROPHETS

"Wherefore by their fruits ye shall know them. Not everyone that saith unto me, Lord, Lord, shall enter into the kingdom of heaven; but he that doeth the will of my Father which is in heaven. Many will say to me in that day, Lord, Lord, have we not prophesied in thy name? and in thy name have cast out devils? and in thy name done many wonderful works? And then will I profess unto them, I never knew you: depart from me, ye that work iniquity" (Matthew 7:20-23). The use of ESP to perform miracles by so-called prophets for show-off and monetary benefit is like invoking strange fire into the temple of the Holy Spirit.

This practice amounts to deception and blaspheming to God Almighty. Those who are truly called by God into the ministry of the gospel will never lack divine supply and

God's backing each time they call upon His name. Not our own will but His will must be done at all times to escape divine indignation of God "And Nadab and Abihu, the sons of Aaron, took either of them his censer, and put fire therein, and put incense thereon, and offered strange fire before the Lord, which he commanded them not. And there went out fire from the Lord, and devoured them, and they died before the Lord. Then Moses said unto Aaron, this is it that the Lord spake, saying, I will be sanctified in them that come nigh me, and before all the people I will be glorified. And Aaron held his peace" (Leviticus 10:1-3).

God is more powerful than mortal man thinks and He does not need the carnal help of man to carry out His divine purposes on earth. He would be glorified in the life and ministry of His faithful ministers who walk in holiness and righteousness of life. This means that obeying God, following His direction and doing his perfect will is the secret of a successful and rewarding ministry. Here is what God says concerning the deceptive minister of the gospel. "Cursed be he that doeth the work of the LORD deceitfully, and cursed be he that keepeth back his sword from blood" (Jeremiah 48:10).

ESP is meant to identify the underlying physical or emotional conditions. A psychic channelling is the activation of one's awareness to receive a flow of intuitive information and communication by aligning with thoughts and feelings of the individual and seeing into the future. The process and ability to receive information is independent of the five senses of man. It is a special sense beyond vision, hearing, smell, touch and taste with unlimited range through thought. The types are:

- **Clairvoyance** – The means of seeing events or objects happening somewhere else.
- **Mediumship** – The channelling of dead spirits.
- **Precognition** – The means of seeing the future.
- **Psychometry** – The means of reading about a person or place by touching a physical object.
- **Telepathy** – The means of reading another's thoughts.
- **Retrocognition** – The means of seeing into the distant past.
- **Telekinesis** – The means of altering the physical world with mind power alone.

Of a truth, the above-mentioned are said to be used for good purposes but it is not all things that look good to man that are acceptable in the sight of God. Prophets of God cannot use any of these demonic means in disguise or as an alternative to the miracle power of God. Prophecy is not a Christian alternative to fortune-telling. In most cases, false prophets use these tricks to deceive many people in the church today. Some ministers use charms to make people fall under the 'anointing' (annoying thing in God's sight) and make them roll on the floor as if miracles are happening. Some of these prophets produce soap that can supposedly wash away sins more than the blood of Jesus Christ. Be not deceived, there are many such spirits and people in the world today that falsely claim to be from God with all their damnable heresies but they are not!

"But there were false prophets also among the people, even as there shall be false teachers among you, who privily shall bring in damnable heresies, even denying the Lord that bought them, and bring upon themselves swift destruction. And many shall follow their pernicious ways; by reason of whom the way of truth shall be evil spoken of. And through covetousness shall they with feigned words make merchandise of you: whose judgment now of a long time lingereth not, and their damnation slumbereth not" (2 Peter 2:1-3).

Many worshippers that are falling as prey under the deception of operational gifts which people refer to as fallen under the anointing (or annoy-thing in God's presence) mistakenly claim that it is the supernatural acts of God. During the earthly ministry of our Lord Jesus Christ, He warned every believer to "beware of false prophets" (Mathew 7:15-20) who always dress in sheep's clothing to deceive. When God led Israel out of Egypt through the leadership of Moses, there arose false prophets among the people who later became so prominent among God's people to the extent that kings need to consult them for direction before going to war against their enemy nations.

Those false prophets among God's people operate by the spirit of manipulation, divination, lying spirit, with magic and evil powers to perform the supernatural acts of their master, Satan with lying wonders to deceive people that come to them (1 Kings 22:21-23). Unfortunately, born again Christians, even the very elect of God, can be deceived if they fail to be watchful and prayerful!

These are the Last Days indeed. There are false signs and wonders, fake prophecies and deceptive miracles from the devil. The activities of false prophets are on the increase today. Lying wonders are the tricks of Satan to deceive; hence believers are admonished not to believe every spirit (1 John 4:1-2). Watch out for the peddlers of these false prophecies. Eternal doom awaits those who are entangled by them. Do not buy their lies because they are poisonous. They have nothing to offer you than false hope. Control your curiosity. Evil prophecies can't profit your life. Seduction is their trademark. Do not be carried away with their sweet promises. Avoid them for the sake of your precious soul. Yes, escape for your life!

WORSHIP OF THE QUEEN OF HEAVEN

"The children gather wood, and the fathers kindle the fire, and the women knead their dough, to make cakes to the queen of heaven, and to pour out drink offerings unto other gods, that they may provoke me to anger" (Jeremiah 7:18). Many are indirectly worshipping the queen of heaven as acclaimed to 'Holy Mary' more than Jesus Himself today since the time of Jeremiah. The idea that Mary (the mother of our Lord Jesus Christ) is the queen of heaven has no Biblical basis. The word of God qualified her as greatly favoured and blessed to be chosen among women to bear the Lord and

Saviour of the world. This other Mary or Semiramis is a demon goddess-queen in heavenly places which is not Biblical but is the crafted doctrine of Popes and priests of the Roman Catholic Church.

In his book, *Satan, the Prince of Darkness*, Dr Frederick A. Tatford submitted that Nimrod (which means "rebel"), the son of Cush and grandson of Ham, one of Noah's three sons (Genesis 10:8-9) brought pagan idolatry traceable to Babylonian mysteries into the limelight and built Babel (which means "confusion") in a plain in Shinar. The royal pair of this dark king Nimrod and his beautiful but infamous wife-queen *Semiramis* and their child became the object of idolatrous worship in very widely separated countries. They strove to emancipate men from the fear of God and old patriarchal faith and induce them to find their chief enjoyment in sensual pleasure. Their worship in latter days was celebrated with Bacchanalian orgies and gross immorality.

Traditions regarding his death are somewhat confused but it appears he was put to death for apostacy. After his death, he was deified under the name of Orion. The object of this religious system was to bind all mankind into blind submission to the idolatrous priesthood with its royal head. At a later date, his widow – *Semiramis* and her child also found a place among the stars of heaven and the worship of the queen of heaven and her babe became almost universal – a diabolical imitation, as it was, of what God had revealed.

Tatford said, when Babylon was destroyed, Pergamos became the centre of false religion; and in the apocalyptic message to the Church of Pergamos, our Lord referred to the throne of Satan being there and to Satan dwelling there (Revelation 2:13). Babylon was the fountain-head of idolatry and the scene of one of Satan's victories. A blow was there struck at the patriarchal faith in God, the effects of which are seen in most of the false religions of the present day.

What exists in Heaven is not a queen of heaven but the KING of kings and the LORD of lords in the Heaven of heavens. God warned the children of Israel by Moses against worshipping the hosts of heaven practiced by the people of Canaan. "And lest thou lift up thine eyes unto heaven, and when thou seest the sun, and the moon, and the stars, even all the host of heaven, shouldest be driven to worship them, and serve them, which the LORD thy God hath divided unto all nations under the whole heaven... And hath gone and served other gods, and worshipped them, either the sun, or moon, or any of the host of heaven, which I have not commanded" (Deuteronomy 4:19; 17:3). From the Scriptural point of view, the queen of heaven originated from pagan Babylonian goddess worship ever since the Old Testament era before Mary. They are:

- Asherah (grove) – Mother goddess of the Canaanites (Exodus 34:11-13; 1 Kings 14:15, 23).
- Ashtoreth - Moon goddess of sexuality and prostitution; wife of Baal (god), also known as Molech (1 Kings 11:33).

- Tammuz – god of fertility of ancient Mesopotamia (Ezekiel 8:13-15).
- Diana (Artemis) – The ancient Roman goddess (Acts 19:23-41).

These are nothing but Polytheistic religions that honour both gods and goddesses together. It is a subtle way of goddess worship but God still remains merciful in all situations, not willing that anyone should perished in the sin of idolatry. He is still sending His faithful messengers to warn His people and turn from the sin of idolatry to worship the only true God but, they refused to listen and continued with their open rebellion against the authority of God.

During Jeremiah's days, this is what the people said. "As for the word that thou hast spoken unto us in the name of the LORD, we will not hearken unto thee. But we will certainly do whatsoever thing goeth forth out of our own mouth, to burn incense unto the queen of heaven, and to pour out drink offerings unto her, as we have done, we, and our fathers, our kings, and our princes, in the cities of Judah, and in the streets of Jerusalem: for then had we plenty of victuals, and were well, and saw no evil" (Jeremiah 44:16-17).

Idolatrous practices of worshipping a deity or demi-god instead of the only true God and building altars to these gods constituted strongholds of ideologies that were opposed to God in all ramifications. These constituted strongholds perfuse our minds and thinking; and we are unshielded from all sorts of mindsets and value systems we presumptuously allow and believe.

There are personal, generational or family, cultural and cosmic strongholds. This is the situation of many people today who imported these ideologies into faith. They put one leg in the church and other leg in the shrine or temple of Satan, yet they still claim that they are ministers of the gospel.

Chapter 4

SUBTLE DEVICES OF SATAN

Satan, the Devil, is full of subtlety of evil devices or tricks. These crafty methods and strategies are contrary to God's plan, purpose and program for humanity but the devil is always looking for opportunity to strike and perpetuate his evil onslaught. "Lest Satan should get an advantage of us: for we are not ignorant of his devices… The thief cometh not, but for steal, and to kill, and to destroy …." (John 10:10). Satan's devices refer to his evil thoughts, purposes, strategies and designs of a master plan of wickedness. The word is translated devices (2 Corinthians 2:11); and minds (2 Corinthians 4:4) and thought (2 Corinthians 10:5). Satan has been in his subtle operation since a very long time ago. He has been achieving his devices against man on the surface of the earth through demon-inspired suggestions and temptations. It takes wisdom, understanding, control and inspiration of God's Spirit to apprehend Satan's subtle devices and to defeat him.

Whatever the devil does against a believer has a sinister purpose. Satan always opposes God's purpose for man and walks in the opposite direction of whatever is God's plan and purpose for His people. As a result, Christians who are engaged in spiritual warfare should be vigilant and cannot afford to be careless about his spiritual life because Satan lurks out there to exploit every available loophole to his own advantage. He looks for every available opportunity to bring believers down by all means. We must not be ignorant of this truth. "Be sober, be vigilant; because your adversary the devil, as a roaring lion, walketh about, seeking whom he may devour: Whom resist steadfast in the faith, knowing that the same afflictions are accomplished in your brethren that are in the world" (1 Peter 5:8-9). Among other things, Satan's uses subtlety for the following reasons:

To steal the joy of God's people, kill their dreams and destroy their lives. He also blinds the minds of sinners to the truth of salvation and hardens the hearts of backsliders to prevent them from being restored to God.

To block blessings and frustrate believers out of God's will and plan.

To influence situations so as to cause Christians to be impatient with God and entice them to take shortcuts that could lead to everlasting sorrow. However, impatience is a mark of unbelief, fleshly desire and immaturity in the life of the erring believer and not part of Satan's devices).

To downgrade God's people to lesser, lower and base levels in the scheme of things.

To deceive people by using fake miracle workers to carry out his onslaught. He attempts to hinder the manifestation of God's glory from shinning in the lives of the saints of God.

From Biblical injunctions and personal Christian experiences in warfare for the past seven years, I can boldly say that spiritual battle is real but God is faithful to deliver His own children. Hence spiritual warfare is real and not a fantasy or mere exaggeration! Evil is prevalent because the devil is at war against humanity! The power of darkness is in serious confrontation with holy and righteous standards! There is war everywhere because Satan is an opposer and a usurper! Enemies can strike at any time using a variety of weapons - disasters, disappointments, destitution, diseases, sadness, sorrow, sufferings, temptations, troubles, torments, tribulations to mention a few!

Many, especially the ignorant ones, have been defeated, disgraced and destroyed for lack of knowledge of spiritual warfare! We need to be rightly informed that Satan and his demons are walking about and looking for whom to disturb, devour and destroy! But the truth is that true Christians can overcome him in all kinds of battles and warfare because they are more than conquerors through Jesus Christ! Every child of God is assured of victory because their weapons of warfare are not carnal but mighty through God to the pulling down of strongholds! Remember you cannot defeat Satan if you are still living in sin or ignorant of his devices! Also, holiness, faith and prayers are needed to overcome this diehard adversary! If you possess these qualities, your victory is assured!

Satan's target of believers is to fight in order to derail them from the purpose of God. In all these, Satan is a loser! - he has never won and he will never win! We shall overcome him through the Captain of our salvation. The description of Satan's devices can be enumerated as follows:

IGNORANCE

The problem that some people have today is the veil of ignorance that is covering their spiritual eyes and many Christians fall into this category. This has given the devil an ample opportunity to take advantage of them. ..."For so is the will of God, that with well doing ye may put to silence the ignorance of foolish men... Having the understanding darkened, being alienated from the life of God through the ignorance that is in them, because of the blindness of their heart...Lest Satan should get an advantage of us: for we are not ignorant of his devices" (1 Peter 2:15; Ephesians 4:18; 2 Corinthians 2:11).

The devil exploits people's ignorance to keep them in perpetual bondage of sins, sicknesses, afflictions, obsession, oppression, possession and failure without realizing it. As a result, they continue to seek help and solution desperately where there is none. This makes many Christians to act independently - outside God's will. This is Satan's craftiness and deception to lure man into sin against God.

The cure for ignorance is to study the Word of God meditatively and prayerfully as described in 2 Timothy 2:15; Proverbs 4:7, "Study to shew thyself approved unto God, a workman that needeth not to be ashamed, rightly dividing the word of truth …Wisdom is the principal thing; therefore get wisdom: and with all thy getting get understanding."

There is much potent understanding that believers could get in the Holy Scriptures that would save them from the trap of the enemy if they take time to study. If they make time to seek for Godly counsel on life matters, this will reduce likely risks and problems! Advice from Godly men can work for you, but, above all, seek counsel from the Word of God and the Holy Spirit! Remember, the word of God is life and spirit; and the Holy Spirit is the Great Teacher and Counsellor.

Counselling from the right and appropriate quarters will build your confidence, reduce likely risks and solve great problems that would have escalated! Honest and earnest adherence to good and Godly counsel will save you from making great mistakes and taking wrong steps. So, always seek for counsel before taking any critical step in life! Maintain a positive relationship with God! Draw closer to Him. Always obey His Word and do His will in all matters and situations - no matter how difficult. Remember that without God, you are nothing and can do nothing! Come to Him with a grateful heart, even when things are not normal or pleasant. Honour Him at all times and you will see Him show up for you in all situations!

FLEETING PLEASURE AND GUILT OF SINS
"By faith Moses, when he was come to years, refused to be called the son of Pharaoh's daughter; Choosing rather to

suffer affliction with the people of God, than to enjoy the pleasures of sin for a season; Esteeming the reproach of Christ greater riches than the treasures in Egypt: for he had respect unto the recompence of the reward" (Hebrews 11:24-26). The tempter entices people with divers kind of lusts and temptations to make them sin and gives them a false assurance that God would always forgive them any time they sin deliberately if they repent after sinning. Those whom Satan cannot keep in ignorance, he entices, twists and leads into error, doctrines of devils and falsehood.

As Satan did to Eve, he is continually seeking for whom to devour. Through his subtlety, he seeks to corrupt our minds from the simplicity that is in Christ. "But shun profane and vain babblings: for they will increase unto more ungodliness. And their word will eat as doth a canker: of whom is Hymenaeus and Philetus; Who concerning the truth have erred, saying that the resurrection is past already; and overthrow the faith of some "(2 Timothy 2:16-18). Satan wants believers to fall and remain in a state of backsliding after the pleasure of sin. He wants them to experience regret and remorse instead of seeking God's face for mercy in true repentance.

One thing the devil does is to tempt Christians to sin and keep accusing them so that they focus their attention on self-pity and the sins they have committed. Satan knows that if they remain in the state of backsliding and regret, they would end up with him in the Lake of Fire. He wants to keep all backsliders and sinners perpetually under the dark cloud of guilt and render them useless and ineffective in the Kingdom of God.

Joseph, in his life time, valued his relationship with God more than temporary and sinful pleasures that Potiphar's wife was offering him (Genesis 39:7-9). He chose to suffer for righteousness sake to inherit the Kingdom of God than to sow to the flesh and reap corruption. "Blessed are they which are persecuted for righteousness' sake: for theirs is the kingdom of heaven…We know that whosoever is born of God sinneth not; but he that is begotten of God keepeth himself, and that wicked one toucheth him not" (Matthew 5:10; 1 John 5:18).

WORLDLINESS AND COMPROMISE

The devil's strategy is to make every believer to compromise the principles of God's truth and righteousness. It's to forfeit our personal conviction in Christ and the standard of God's Word by which we conduct Christian life. "Ye adulterers and adulteresses, know ye not that the friendship of the world is enmity with God? whosoever therefore will be a friend of the world is the enemy of God" (James 4:4). Christians live temporarily in the world ruled by Satan, but they are not a part of the system that opposed God. Salvation transforms our hearts and converts our lives. When Christ comes into the heart, God's power saves us from all sins, old things pass away and all things become new.

Now, the hunger and desire to please the Lord is registered in the heart of such a new born again believer. In the midst of a perverse and crooked world, at home, in business, indeed, everywhere and anywhere, God's people always live for Him. "If ye then be risen with Christ, seek those things which are above, where Christ sitteth on the right hand of God. Set your affection on things above, not on things on the earth" (Colossians 3:1-2).

If our affection is on godly things, our hearts will not be tied or glued to the things of the world. Jesus said and He is still saying that where a man's treasure is, there his heart will be. Those who harbour affection for the world and the things it affords and promises cannot be a true disciple of Jesus Christ. Human thoughts, principles, actions and practices of the world are continually and constantly opposed to the purpose of God. The passion and practice of worldliness is the opposite of God's standard of holiness for heavenly-minded Christians.

Every moment in the life of the worldly person is inclined to the satisfying of sinful desires and pleasures. Those who live and die as part of the world can only hope for everlasting damnation with the devil as enemies of God. Even the devil is fully aware that one of the easiest ways of making the Christian an enemy of God and losing his divine benefits is worldliness or friendship with the world.

By temptation and deception, Satan always tries to offer his own substitute and move us outside of the will of God by a compromise. He uses a cunning alternative. What he offers are the lust of eyes and sensual things that have no eternal value. These are fornication, adultery and instruments of seduction, covetousness and the pride of life among other things. By yielding to any of his provisions, such a saint will automatically grant him access to his possessions. "Take heed, brethren, lest there be in any of you an evil heart of unbelief, in departing from the living God" (Hebrews 3:12).

Children are easy targets of the devil as he is working daily to flood their hearts with the tide of iniquity and evil. Parents should teach and warn their children in connection with pornographic videos, demonic games, cosmic books and magazines, many of which have a definitely strong influence upon their hearts to think and do evil. Separation from the world is a mark of true Christianity! Understand this - you can't be a friend of the world and still love God! No one can serve two masters; he will either hate one or leave the other! Dainties, allurements and attractions of the world are vanity! All that is in the world: the lust of the flesh, the lust of the eyes and the pride of life, is not of God! You cannot serve God and mammon together! Above all, it is the sole responsibility of every believer to work out their own salvation with fear and trembling, that is, with determination to stand firm on the principles of God's truth, come what may!

UNEQUAL YOKE AND EVIL FRIENDSHIP
"Be ye not unequally yoked together with unbelievers: for what fellowship hath righteousness with unrighteousness?

and what communion hath light with darkness? And what concord hath Christ with Belial? or what part hath he that believeth with an infidel? And what agreement hath the temple of God with idols? for ye are the temple of the living God; as God hath said, I will dwell in them, and walk in them; and I will be their God, and they shall be my people. Wherefore come out from among them, and be ye separate, saith the Lord, and touch not the unclean thing; and I will receive you. And will be a Father unto you, and ye shall be my sons and daughters, saith the Lord Almighty (2 Corinthians 6:14-18).

The Lord unmistakably condemns unequal yoke between Christians and unbelievers. The consequence of unequal yoke and evil friendship is an open door of satanic invasion and vulnerability to a steady weakening of one's spiritual foundation that would lead to loss of focus, commitment and consecration to the Lord (Revelation 2:4). Unequal yoke will turn the Lord's face against any Christian who engages in any evil association for any reason. A Christian should pray consistently for more grace and spiritual conviction that would keep him away from compromising any part of God's word in these last days.

We must beware of unequal yoke in friendship selection, marriage partnership, business relationship as these could lead to sinful acts and ungodliness. Church leaders that watch over the flock of God are responsible for keeping the church free from compromise and corruption. As believers, God expects us to take our stand in the midst of a perverse and sinful generation. Christians are chosen from the world to be God's peculiar treasure. At the same time, we should pray for spiritual sensitivity and grace to break away from any blinding relationships that would qualify us as enemies of God. True Christianity is manifested by how we love people, how we keep ourselves pure, how we keep our tongue under control and how we keep ourselves undefiled by the world (James 1:27).

PRAYERLESSNESS AND CARELESSNESS

"Moreover as for me, God forbid that I should sin against the Lord in ceasing to pray for you: but I will teach you the good and the right way" (1 Samuel 12:23). Prayerlessness will lead to lukewarmness and lethargy. It is a sin that separates us from achieving God's purpose for our lives and the Kingdom of God. Once the spiritual life of a prayerless Christian dies out, he is unfruitful, careless and useless to the things of God. No useless person has a space in Heaven because they would be spewed out of God's Kingdom and lose all its benefits and rewards.

Prayerlessness would lead to problems with the flesh as a prayerless and godless person easily becomes a prey to Satan's influence and manipulation. It is an act of disobeying Christ's word and a sign of following Him at a distance way far off. "And he spake a parable unto them to this end, that men ought always to pray, and not to faint" (Luke 18:1). Prayerless believers would be careless with their Christian lives. One can only pray rightly when one is watchful enough to discern what is necessary in prayer for the Christian life, aspiration and God's service.

Show me a man who has vision for mission and I will show you a man who is passionate with burdened heart and bended kneels. Never give up! Each time you get discouraged and give up, Satan rejoices! Believe in yourself and put your trust in God! Remember, nothing can stop you except you stop yourself! Until you finish, do not hang the glove or throw in the towel! Put in more efforts! All tasks that you finished started in your mind ever before you began it! Resist all forms of discouragement! It is a spirit! Yes, receive the grace to continue in prayers and finish what you have started, so that you can testify and celebrate.

PROLIFERATION OF FALSE RELIGIONS

The proliferation of false religions and practices is a satanic device and project meant to exchange the true God for a false god or gods more than ever before in these last days. "For such are false apostles, deceitful workers, transforming themselves into the apostles of Christ. And no marvel; for Satan himself is transformed into an angel of light. Therefore, it is no great thing if his ministers also be transformed as the ministers of righteousness; whose end shall be according to their works" (2 Corinthians 11:13-15).

The greatest device which Satan uses to get people down is false religions and practices as bait to blind them to the truth and salvation. Many so-called ministers of the gospel are mixing pop psychology, philosophies, religious idea, tradition and spirituality with the Bible message today. These practices are falsehood and the tricks of Satan to keep man in perpetual bondage. It is all a calculated attempt to exchange the true God for something otherwise which somewhat resembles Him. How do we recognize these false religions in our society? Any religion practices that confess not that Jesus Christ as Son of God sent to the world to save humanity from the power of sins and its consequences is not of God (1 John 5:12). Shedding an innocent blood or ritual killings for the sake of religion is not the act of God but Satan (Psalms 106:38; James 1:27). Those who live by the world's principles and philosophies are friends of the world and are enemies of God. The lifestyle of a true man must be according to the Word of God as declared by the Holy Bible.

INCITEMENT OF PERSECUTION AGAINST CHRIS-TIANS
"Fear none of those things which thou shalt suffer: behold, the devil shall cast some of you into prison, that ye may be tried; and ye shall have tribulation ten days: be thou faithful unto death, and I will give thee a crown of life. He that hath an ear, let him hear what the Spirit saith unto the churches; He that overcometh shall not be hurt of the second death" (Revelation 2:10-11). The source of persecution against the church of the living God is Satan. He always opposes and fights anything related to God, most especially in the area of salvation of souls. Once you declare your loyalty with Jesus Christ, Satan hates your new life in Christ and will stir up the fire of persecution against you. The reason for persecution is to frustrate and discourage such a Christian from following the Lord Jesus Christ. If they refused to be

discouraged, Satan will not hesitate to instigate his agents against them to be killed.

The killings of Christians and burning of churches from opposing religions all over the world are masterminded by the devil. Persecution measures our faith in God in every situation and Jesus Christ had foreseen that these would happen to His followers. He has this to say to encourage and strengthen believers on how to stand against the onslaught of persecution being levelled against them by the enemy of their souls. "Blessed are they which are persecuted for righteousness' sake: for theirs is the kingdom of heaven. Blessed are ye, when men shall revile you, and persecute you, and shall say all manner of evil against you falsely, for my sake. Rejoice, and be exceeding glad: for great is your reward in heaven: for so persecuted they the prophets which were before you" (Matthew 5:10-12).

For all Christians, trials and temptations are real and inevitable, no matter your degree or level of faith! Honestly, your faith will be tried! However, you need to understand that all these are not to crush you but to make you stronger! Remember, Jesus said, you shall have tribulations. "These things I have spoken unto you, that in me ye might have peace. In the world ye shall have tribulation: but be of good cheer; I have overcome the world" (John16:33)! So, expect their doses; Determine to overcome! Ask God for more grace! Yield not to sin and do not faint; but pray "But they that wait upon the LORD shall renew their strength; they shall mount up with wings as eagles; they shall run, and not be weary; and they shall walk, and not faint" (Isaiah 40:31).

Do not justify temptation: it is an experience that is common to all humans - saints and sinners, old and young, illiterates and elites! All mortal men are prone to temptation and no one has immunity over it, but it can be escaped or overcome. Never underestimate or gloss over it; temptation can come to you both in private and in the public or anywhere at any time! On the flip side, temptation is a challenging companion but a bad friend. It can bite you hard if you fall into it. Yielding to it can bring you down to shame. Always have the consciousness that temptation itself is not a sin but it is an enticement to sin or do evil. Yielding to temptation is what definitely becomes a sin.

Regardless of your status, the tempter will always target you and set you up and no one falls into temptation without being lustful first. A bird can freely fly above your head but you can disallow it from making a nest on your head. You can overcome temptation through the Word of God, watchfulness and being prayerful. If you keep the Word of God, He also will keep you in the hour of your temptation!

Chapter 5

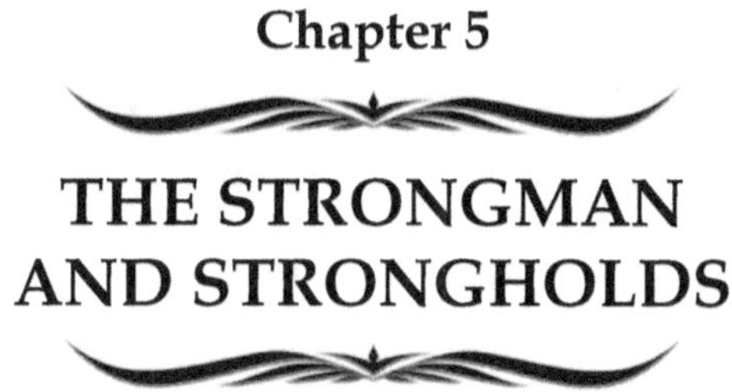

THE STRONGMAN AND STRONGHOLDS

"No man can enter into a strong man's house, and spoil his goods, except he will first bind the strong man; and then he will spoil his house… For though we walk in the flesh, we do not war after the flesh: (For the weapons of our warfare are not carnal, but mighty through God to the pulling down of strong holds;) Casting down imaginations, and every high thing that exalteth itself against the knowledge of God, and bringing into captivity every thought to the obedience of Christ; And having in a readiness to revenge all disobedience, when your obedience is fulfilled" (Mark 3:27; 2 Corinthians 10:3-6).

Satan is the strong man who possesses his agents or works in human beings by means of evil spirits to carry out acts of wickedness. The nature of Satan's craftiness and deception can be seen in the activities of his agents assigned to destroy life and destiny. Moreover, the strongman is a satanic agent and assailant of high rank in the demonic kingdom who creates confusion, spiritual problems and sicknesses that defy solution. He operates from inside the invisible fortress which Satan builds in man's life.

A stronghold may be a thought, false notion, influence or ideology used by the devil to keep people in bondage. It is a fortified defence base of operation for the strongman to carry out his offensive attacks against anyone. Moreover, strongholds are a collection of ideas, arguments and thoughts in harmony with Satan's lies and principles which are always averse to the truth. Ideological strongholds originate from the carnal mind and are rooted in the depraved nature of man to proliferate false religions, terrorism, superstitions, erroneous beliefs and destructive philosophies. It holds victims strongly as captives to sinful lifestyles.

The strongman is a satanic general that has demons under his control, authority and sphere of influence to wreak havoc in believers' lives. The Lord Jesus described the attitude and characteristics of the strongman - when he possesses a man, he is fully-armed to guard and to keep his victims strictly in perpetual captivity. This means that the strongman blinds the thought life and thinking faculty of unbelievers or his victims against the gospel of salvation that has the greater power to liberate from sins, self (human nature), Satan, sickness and the world. We can also describe the strongman as a volunteer of Satan who is saturated with evil powers to attack, devour and destroy fellow human beings diabolically.

From my personal experience and divine revelation given to me, some of these agents of Satan have satanic names in the realm of the spirit. We may be seeing them physically as fellow human beings, but they are actually generations of vipers in the real life. Some strongmen who are human agents of Satan transform themselves spiritually into strange birds in the night, cats, snakes, serpents, tigers, lions or other animals and beasts to carry out nefarious assignments of destroying lives and destinies. Through deception and manipulation, they gain access and exercise full control over the minds of people who are sincerely ignorant of their diabolical ways. Through the spirit of lying, familiar spirit, divinations and sorceries, however, they can demonically see the future of their prospective victims and block opportunities coming their ways. They hinder success, steal, kill and destroy lives and properties of susceptible colleagues, neighbours, friends and other human beings.

Satanic-strongmen are high-ranking satanic officers and officials who are very deceptive in nature, destructive in operation and deadly. They are diabolical and demonically empowered to create problems, cause confusion, create division and manipulate people's mind in a crafty manner so as to gain total control of their lives. The strongman is a tyrant and the way of peace is far from him. But as Satan possesses his agents to wreak havoc with evil spirits, so also, the Lord Jesus Christ has always given the power of the Holy Ghost to possess all who have given their lives to Him. They have a greater power than Satan to set the captives free! "Behold, I give unto you power to tread on serpents and scorpions, and over all the power of the enemy: and nothing shall by any means hurt you... Verily I say unto you, Whatsoever ye shall bind on earth shall be bound in heaven: and whatsoever ye shall loose on earth shall be loosed in heaven" (Luke 10:19; Matthew 18:18).

Whatever believers bind on earth through the name of Jesus shall be bound in heaven and anything we shall loose on earth shall also be loosed in heaven; and when we decree a thing, it shall be established. It behoves every child of God to put on the whole armour of God and activate them through the life of obedience and prayers to be able to pull down the strongholds of Satan and do exploits in God's Kingdom. The spirit of the devil is rebellious and disobedient and the good Lord is ready to revenge all disobedience when our own obedience to God's word is fulfilled. Then, strongholds shall be knocked down in your life and family. This makes it difficult for such strongholds to operate in any area of your life.

The prevailing hands of God shall destabilize and overpower them. There shall be no power of darkness that will be able to stand before you. All their attempts and plans shall be subdued on your behalf. Move yourself closer to the Lord of lords at whose name every knee bows and do not be afraid of their terrorism and intimidation any longer. Enough of such intimidation over your life and family! Resist all forces and powers that may want to dominate any area of your life henceforth in the name of Jesus!

LYING SPIRIT

"Lying lips are abomination to the LORD: but they that deal truly are his delight" (Proverbs 12:22). Our Heavenly Father is the God of truth and the Lord Jesus Christ is the way, the truth and the life. Even the Holy Spirit is the Spirit of truth. Therefore, in the Kingdom of God, there is no room for any child of God or a Christian to tell lies for any reason. Telling lies is a sin and an abomination to God, but for Satan, his agents and unbelievers, it is normal. Some call it the new normal or alternative facts. Rather, God calls it the way of this present world under the control of Satan.

It is part of the activities of satanic strongmen to control and encourage lying which the Lord abhors such as the spirit of deception, hypocrisy, falsehood, wrong doctrines, false religions, guile, craftiness of any kind, exaggeration, flattery, slander, destructive gossip, unkind criticism and sinful diplomacy anywhere and at all times.

Jesus denounced the spirit of lying in His earthly ministry when He vehemently told the Jews, "Ye are of your father the devil, and the lusts of your father ye will do. He was a murderer from the beginning, and abode not in the truth, because there is no truth in him. When he speaketh a lie, he speaketh of his own: for he is a liar, and the father of it" (John 8:44; Please read Proverbs 6:16-19).

Compulsive lying is a lifestyle of the people controlled by lying demons in customized ways. Such people are demonically obsessed to tear people down through lying and tell lies with fluency as if they are speaking their own native language. They are extremely defiant and rebellious to God's word, hateful towards the truth and spiteful of those that are good. Always remember that a faithful witness of Christ does not lie but a false witness and an ambassador of the kingdom of darkness thrive in lies. It is imperative for a child of God to speak the truth in all situations, defend the truth and if necessary, die for the truth. Telling the truth at all times reveals the quality of our love towards God and humanity. This showcases a life of true Christian value and virtue.

Believers are not to believe every spirit because not all spirits are of God (1 John 4:1-6). With the help of the Holy Spirit, we can discern and differentiate between the Spirit of truth and the lying spirit. Today, false prophets operating with lying spirits of the devil are on rampage in every street to deceive. We should turn deaf ears to diviners and those false prophets who are always out to use magical powers to perform miracles. Their prophecy may come to pass, their visions may be real, they may be going up and down with big Bibles and speaking in tongues with superficial meekness and charismatic smiles but it is all to seduce and deceive.

I remember a woman who visited our church when I was pastoring in the country of my birth. This woman was having high blood pressure and requested for prayers and counselling. During the course of our discussion, I asked this woman what steps she had taken so far in finding a solution to her ordeal. She showed me the medications and went on to explain how she visited one prophet who introduced to her for prayer of healing and deliverance. After the prayer, this woman said she forgot her headscarf in the office of the so-called prophet. This prophet did not know that the woman forgot her headscarf in his office. When the woman came back to the office to pick her stuff, she saw the prophet reciting incantations with animal's horn in his hand. The reaction of the prophet was outrageous against the woman because he was caught red-handed using demonic power for prophecy and miracles.

The Bible has this to say, "To the law and to the testimony: if they speak not according to this word, it is because there is no light in them" (Isaiah 8:20). Evil spirits are not far from any man of God in title who finds it so easy to lie with all diverse weights, deceits, false teaching, fake prophecy, slander, negative gossip, self-deception, wrong accusations, covenant breaking, sensual emotional actions, pretence and perilous perversions. All these behavioural footholds build up in the mind to become a satanic stronghold in the life of all liars. "…and all liars, shall have their part in the lake which burneth with fire and brimstone: which is the second death" (Revelation 21:8).

SPIRIT OF FEAR

"For God hath not given us the spirit of fear; but of power, and of love, and of a sound mind" (2 Timothy 1:7). This verse of the Scriptures confirmed that the spirit of fear is not from God. Fear is the basic human emotion that gives the devil an opportunity to gain access into man's life. The spirit of fear manifests in anxiety, compulsive behavioural patterns, terror, panic, insomnia, nightmare, anguish and phobias, which can lead to heart attack, cardiac arrest, fear of man and fear of death. Job said, "For the thing which I greatly feared is come upon me, and that which I was afraid of is come unto me" (Job 3:25). Many people are victims of fear of the unknown that has given the devil room to attack them freely. God knows the tricks of the devil and warned, "fear not," that appeared about three hundred and sixty-five times on the pages of the Scriptures. Anyone who operates in the spirit of fear cannot please God. If you love God and trust Him, you cannot exercise fear in the midst of storms of life (1 John 4:18).

Fear is the opposite of faith. It suppresses and subjects you to focus on problems rather than on the God of solutions. Fear is an enemy and a robber that steals your peace and joy if you entertain it! Fear is a deceiver and liar with a smooth and velvet tongue. Fear is a tyrant that always tells you to run. Experiences that are not real are what fear triggers and promotes, but God has not given us the spirit of fear, rather, He has given us the spirit of love, power and sound mind! Understand, fear is a spirit and it is called 'False Experience Appearing Real!' Ask for boldness from the Lord and command all forms of fear to leave you, in Jesus Name!

Regardless of your situation or experience, always remember that all things are possible with God! Yes, anything that is not of faith is sin! Doubt and unbelief bring fear! Anxieties and worries are products of fear! Get rid of them through the prayer of faith today! Fear negatively impacts health, causes the heart to race, makes the eyes to dilate and the entire body tense to vibrate. We quickly forgot that fear is the access door for Satan to inflict us with injury and pain. The best men can also be prone to fear. The devil preys on people by promoting their fears as he did to Job.

Except we harbour fear like Job, Satan has no power to attack you; even if he does, God has the power to drive it out as we pray in faith. The antidote to fear remains faith, your faith grows as you believe in God and His promises. When you feed your faith, your fear shall be starved to death!

On the flip side, there is the fear that is needful. It can be found in the book of Ecclesiastes 12:13-14, "Let us hear the conclusion of the whole matter: Fear God, and keep his commandments: for this is the whole duty of man. For God shall bring every work into judgment, with every secret thing, whether it be good, or whether it be evil." Those who have given their life to Jesus Christ love and appreciate the provisions of God's work of grace with honour and fear. This fear is not the slavish type that would make someone perceive God as a taskmaster ready to apply His rod of discipline at every mistake. No, it is a healthy and reverential fear that honours God.

This is Godly fear that is born out of reverence and impulsive worth of respect for the God of all creation at salvation. Just as the Bible explained it in Hebrews 12:28, "Wherefore we receiving a kingdom which cannot be moved, let us have grace, whereby we may serve God acceptably with reverence and godly fear." Our life should be completely dedicated in full of adoration, love and obedience to God's Word. This type of fear is the beginning of wisdom and understanding. No matter a believer's position and past relationship with God, they must understand that God is a consuming fire and would visit the transgressors who deliberately yield to the temptation of the devil and deliberately sin against the God of holiness and righteousness. It is this fear that restraints true believers from sliding into sin. It is the fear of God and not the fear man (Proverbs 1:7; 9:10; Job 28:28).

The fear of God is a sign of reverence and obedience! However, the fear of men or Satan brings a snare! Upholding God's standards gives assurance and hope! Reverencing God is a mark of strength! Slavish fear puts one in a cage of ignorance and doubt! Dealing with God emboldens and drives away negative fears! As you grow in the Lord, He grants you more grace for victory over other fears. Yes, fear God and do not fear men or Satan! Fear God above humans and persons! Serve Him and worship only. Everyone who is proud, haughty and lifted up cannot enjoy the blessings of the Lord. Bring yourself low before God so that He can lift you up in due season!

Receive the grace to regard and respect God above all humans and any mortal! Trust and obey Him with all your mind, heart and soul! Always put first things first, that is, God first! Reach forth to God in prayers concerning your needs. Don't depend on man that would promise and fail. You can never miss God's blessings in your life if you will love Him, walk in His ways, trust Him and fear Him above all humans and persons! Join your faith with Christ so that you can resist and overcome all forms of dream killers. Avoid and resist fear, threats, discouragement, doubt, unbelief, disappointment and other dream killers.

Never yield to the temptation of allowing anyone or anything to make you give up on your dream. You must understand that Satan can use your relations, friends, colleagues and family members to cripple your dream! Don't give up. Always focus on how to make your dream work. Keep your dream alive and active. Even at the point of confusion, you must be resolute. Remember, your dream will take you to your next level this year, so, don't allow dream killers to kill it. You are the chief determinant and architect to make your dream count, work and succeed; so, guide it jealously. Always look up unto Jesus for help at your crossroads. I pray for you that your dream will manifest in Jesus' Name.

Keep moving (Exodus 14:15). Surely, no one can stop your journey to the Promised Land. The unforeseen hands of God will always protect and preserve you against all dangers. Nothing will stop you from getting to the land of your dreams! Demons and the hosts of hell cannot stop you. Always focus on God and seek His face for help over all forms of challenges. You will never miss your itinerary to Canaan Land, in Jesus' name.

SPIRIT OF PRIDE

"The fear of the LORD is to hate evil: pride, and arrogancy, and the evil way, and the froward mouth, do I hate…Judge not, that ye be not judged. For with what judgment ye judge, ye shall be judged: and with what measure ye mete, it shall be measured to you again. And why beholdest thou the mote that is in thy brother's eye, but considerest not the beam that is in thine own eye? Or how wilt thou say to thy brother, let me pull out the mote out of thine eye; and, behold, a beam is in thine own eye? Thou hypocrite, first cast out the beam out of thine own eye; and then shalt thou see clearly to cast out the mote out of thy brother's eye" (Proverbs 8:13; Matthew 7:1-5).

Pride is obsessive attention to self and exaggeration of a person's self-worth. It leads to spiritual decline that manifests in oppression of the poor, materialism, immorality and worldliness. No proud person is a true believer as God resists the proud while He gives grace to the humble. Humility is the key to God's presence and blessings.

Subtle pride: This is an untoward attitude that criticizes negatively and passes judgement on others. It is something of the heart that seeks to tear down, condemn and destroy others with words by speaking of others' sin with contempt and belittling their persons. The causes of pride are evil thoughts, deceits, covetousness, envy and slander in the heart. People with this nature are critical and judgmental. This contradicts the word of God that commanded us to love our neighbours as ourselves and thereby displeases Him. Pride led to Lucifer's demotion. The proud never gets far; their over-bloated impression always turns out to be their calamity. Pride is borne out of ulterior motives and attitude.

Defensiveness: This is an attempt to answer back. Debates, counter claims, arguments and defensive speech pertaining to self is nothing but the work of the flesh. In this situation, such people lack the grace to be silent in the midst of provocation. "But the people held their peace, and answered him not a word: for the king's commandment was, saying, Answer him not" (2 Kings 18:36).

Fault-finding: Fault-finders always come to look for the imperfection of others and they overlook their own faults. As declared, "There is a generation that are pure in their own eyes, and yet is not washed from their filthiness" (Proverbs 30:12). Fault-finders always have a 'holier than thou' attitude but their lives are filled with hypocrisy. They are religious yet wicked, cruel, injurious and evil. They pride themselves in their traditional mode of worship, yet their hearts and mind are not clean because they are not converted. They need the miracle of salvation to escape God's impending judgement.

Jettison all forms of conflict, crisis, misunderstanding, acrimony, rift and bitter quarrel. Avoid anger, hatred, bitterness, malice, revenge and retaliation. Anger rests in the bosom of fools! Take note that bitterness, malice and hatred are dangerous to the peace of your heart! So, avoid them! Unforgiveness is a sin that God hates!

God wants you to forgive your offenders and their offences. Resolve offences before it is too late! All forms of rifts, bitter arguments and disagreements are to be avoided. Seek peace and pursue it for blessed are the peacemakers! Remember, God hates sin and cannot walk with sinners! Anger, hatred, malice, bitterness and acrimony are sins that are punishable by God, so, repent of them. You are to follow peace with all men and holiness without which no man shall see the Lord. Learn to forgive offences so that God too can forgive you! Peace is good for your health and fosters a happy relationship with others.

The tempter is ever near (1 Peter 5:8-9; 1 Chronicles 21:1-4; Job 1:7; Matthew 4:3; James 1:12-15) Watch out! Everyone is tempted when drawn away by his own lust. Divine instruction and warning is, 'Watch.' No one is immune from temptation. Enticement is a major tool Satan uses and he can go to any length to tempt you. Determine not to bow to the devil's suggestion. Always watch unto prayers! Yes, don't yield. Be discerning, sober and vigilant.

Presumption: A state of being arrogant and pretentious. It is a footstep of Satan trying to equate himself with God Almighty. It is the act of arrogating to themselves the authority to change or remove the ancient landmark of God to please self. In Exodus 21:14, the Lord condemned presumption or careless assumption. "But if a man come presumptuously upon his neighbour, to slay him with guile; thou shalt take him from mine altar, that he may die." It is an intentional sin that makes him to lay wait with craftiness in order to carry out his evil intention. This is not an emotional wrong but a deliberate act of planning to commit sin (Read Numbers 15:30).

Self-recognition and attention: These are products of pride. His thoughts are inclined to glorify man, not God. Seeking one's own glory is a satanic ambition that would result into negative consequences and wrath of God. "For I say, through the grace given unto me, to every man that is among you, not to think of himself more highly than he ought to think; but to think soberly, according as God hath dealt to every man the measure of faith" (Romans 12:3). Satan was created beautifully and anointed by God to become one of the chief angels, whose wing covered God's throne in Heaven (Isaiah 14:12-18). He grew proud and attempted to overthrow God Almighty. In the same vain, Nebuchadnezzar embraced the example of self-exaltation and self-praise. His language revealed the pride in his heart (Daniel 4:30). He was not spared by God from being punished as well. Therefore, don't wait for God to humble you but humble yourself.

Despising others: Contemptuous and self-righteous people are proud and without the grace of God. There is no grace for the proud, as their thoughts are deceptive, critical and far above others in self-styled holiness and self-righteous living. "And as the ark of the LORD came into the city of David, Michal Saul's daughter looked through a window, and saw king David leaping and dancing before the LORD; and she despised him in her heart" (2 Samuel 6:16; Read Luke 18:9-14). Proud people despise God's wisdom and instruction and so, despise lawful authority and their fellowmen. Pride is an attitude of independence from God. This is related to arrogance, wickedness, foolishness, scoffing and haughtiness which oppose humility, meekness, fear of God and absolute trust in God. He is proud in his superiority, achievement, morality and self-obsession.

Nevertheless, God is full of mercy and compassion to save the proud if he repents today. Our humble Saviour suffered to bear the sins of humanity and substitute Himself for the proud. All that the proud need to do is to confess his pride with humble faith in our humble Lord and Saviour Jesus Christ. Such would be forgiven of their sins of pride and be translated into the marvellous light of His kingdom.

Superficiality: It is the act of empty profession of Christianity without the true righteousness of God in the life of such an individual. There is negligence of godly convictions and sound doctrines with more attention in self-righteousness, church attendance, payment of tithes and offerings and observance of ordinances without the corresponding life that is free from sin and iniquity. However, it is God's perfect will for us to daily examine ourselves in God's Word and be freed from all sins and its consequences. "Examine yourselves, whether ye be in the faith; prove your own selves. Know ye not your own selves, how that Jesus Christ is in you, except ye be reprobates?" (2 Corinthians 13:5). Flee pride, it destroys! Always remember that pride brought Satan low! In God's presence, a proud person is an abomination! Destruction awaits the proud! Avoid pride in your life! Yes, God resists the proud!

REBELLIOUS SPIRIT

"For rebellion is as the sin of witchcraft, and stubbornness is as iniquity and idolatry. Because thou hast rejected the word of the Lord, he hath also rejected thee from being king" (1 Samuel 15:23). Rebellion is a strong opposition to the authority of God and man. It is a product of unbelief, pride, self-management, presumption which manifests in any resistance to God's will and constituted authority. When children rebelled against their parents (spiritual and natural), they were rebelling against the authority of God over them. People no longer wish to be governed by those in authority assigned over them. They want to have their ways and get things done as they like it. As a result, they defy God's laws and authority constantly. A proud person wants recognition by all means and always seeks to be worshiped, honoured and obeyed like Satan.

Rebellion grieves the heart of God and causes Him to bring severe punishment to the rebel if he refuses to repent. "Now Korah, the son of Izhar, the son of Kohath, the son of Levi, and Dathan and Abiram, the sons of Eliab, and On, the son of Peleth, sons of Reuben, took men: And they rose up before Moses, with certain of the children of Israel, two hundred and fifty princes of the assembly, famous in the congregation, men of renown: And they gathered themselves together against Moses and against Aaron, and said unto them, Ye take too much upon you, seeing all the congregation are holy, every one of them, and the Lord is among them: wherefore then lift ye up yourselves above the congregation of the Lord? And when Moses heard it, he fell upon his face" (Numbers 16:1-4).

These three men accused Moses and Aaron wrongly that they usurped the power of the priesthood leadership over the congregation. Moses, the meek servant of God, couldn't defend himself and humbly fell on his face to request for God's direction and sent for these three men to resolve whatever might be the cause of their grievances but they refused his invitation. This act of defiance towards an authority could result in division, schism, insurrection, revolt and segregation of the people of God within the church. As a result, God decided to bring down His judgement upon them.

As usual, Moses and Aaron interceded for these rebellious leaders (Numbers 16:22). Such a meek person with shepherd's heart like Moses is very scarce to come by today in the congregation of saints. It is very important to know that it was God Himself that conducted their vivisepulture by causing the ground to split open and swallow these rebels alive, not Moses. They were buried alive because they had problem with submitting to constituted authority! Of course, the judgement upon them is being used by apostate leaders to justify themselves from being challenged in spite of their sinful acts to God's word. Therefore, with all impunity, they preach this message on the pulpit to instill negative fears in the hearts of the congregation and force them to compromise with him and silence their good conscience.

If any church member challenges the evil act of these wild shepherds, such would be subject to persecution, and oppression; and would be abused and attacked mentally, verbally and spiritually with all sorts of weapons. An anointed man of God is humble enough to take to correction and always ready to do what God commands. A professed religious leader or apostate who is doctrinally deviant, lacks anointing but has only the annoying thing from Satan and has a rebellious heart only loves to play the religious game and make an outward show of piety. Hence rebellion is a sin against God that attracts the two-edged sword of God's judgement on whosoever offends.

It is a sin unto God to contemn an innocent leader appointed by God and at the same time, it is sinful for leaders to use their position of authority to abuse the members under them financially, morally, mentally and sexually. God's word says: "and, ye fathers, provoke not your children to wrath: but bring them up in the nurture and admonition of the Lord" (Ephesians 6:4). Provocation from the leader against church members is an abuse and a misuse of leadership position which is equivalent to the sin of rebellion against God and His word. No leader or member of any congregation is excluded from the punishment of the sin of rebellion, "…rebellion is as the sin of witchcraft." We are commanded to shun it. Therefore, we can't compare ourselves to Moses or be more concerned with another person's rebellious attitude than ourselves until we are firstly concerned about our own condition and how to get this nature of Satan uprooted from our life. To eschew rebellion, we must guide our hearts with all diligence and ensure that no root of bitterness against God's command or His servants springs up from within to defile us.

PERVERSE SPIRIT

"He that walketh in his uprightness feareth the LORD: but he that is perverse in his ways despiseth him" (Proverbs 14:2). Perverse spirit is the spirit behind filthy thoughts and filthiness, seduction and sexual bondage, unfaithfulness and wickedness, abortion and child abuse, profanity and pornography, false doctrine and atheism. Because of the reprobate mind of the people of Egypt, God Himself permit a perverse spirit to mingle in their midst (Isaiah 19:14). Hence a perverse spirit causes perverted thinking that twists the truth in their mind. There is a perverse gospel that some so-called ministers of God are preaching in this end time with severe consequences from the Lord (Galatians 1:6-9). This situation calls for total repentance of sins, restitution, binding the spirit of perversion and casting it out in the name of Jesus. Pray for total washing, purging and purification by the Blood of Jesus and the power of Holy Ghost.

SPIRIT OF HEAVINESS

"To appoint unto them that mourn in Zion, to give unto them beauty for ashes, the oil of joy for mourning, the garment of praise for the spirit of heaviness; that they might be called trees of righteousness, the planting of the LORD, that he might be glorified" (Isaiah 61:3). Heaviness in man's life is a situation of feeling overwhelmed, frustrated, anxious, discouraged, des-pondent, insomniac and trapped with the burdens of life and negative situations that contend against a person. Also, it may be either you are focusing on your own faults or the faults of other people who hurt you.

It is the habit of fault finding. If not checked, it can degenerate to inner hurt, depression and suicidal thoughts. The spirit of heaviness is from Satan that gains entrance through what you focus on and your thought process. It makes vision blurred to the point that you begin to see yourself in a hopeless situation that would douse your faith in God. Heaviness is like a plague that isolates, makes us feel rejected and steals our joy.

Always remember that Satan hates you as a Christian and it is part of his devices to send the spirit of heaviness to attack your faith. In this situation, it is almost difficult to pray, however, the best weapon to combat the spirit of heaviness is to put on the garment of praises and thanksgiving with melodious songs from the heart. "Speaking to yourselves in Psalms and hymns and spiritual songs, singing and making melody in your heart to the Lord" (Ephesians 5:19). This is what the devil does not want you to do because God inhabits the praises of His people. When you begin to worship and praise God, your Jericho wall begins to collapse, your prison gates opens, God sets ambushments against the power that is trying to hold you captives and victory becomes your portion in Jesus' mighty name! Don't ever allow the spirit of heaviness to rule and hold you captive. In any situation, you can be set free by the power of Jesus Christ today. "The Spirit of the Lord is upon me, because he hath anointed me to preach the gospel to the poor; he hath sent me to heal the brokenhearted, to preach deliverance to the captives, and recovering of sight to the blind, to set at liberty them that are bruised, To preach the acceptable year of the Lord" (Luke 4:18).

Jesus has come to set us free and we shall be free indeed! Of course, if God created you in the womb of your mother and supervised your safe delivery, there is nothing He cannot do for you, if only you will cooperate with Him. Come to think of it, being your Creator, He has full details about your life. If you align with His redemption plan, He cannot leave you or forget you. There is nothing God cannot do to change the story of your life for good! He can take you from the valley to the mountain top. Often times, we want to choose shortcuts towards achieving our goals, not knowing that God's plan is the best for us if only we can wait for His own time and not be fixated on our own time. Believe it or not, God is able to do new things in your life provided you can hand over yourself to Him and commit the affairs of your life into His hands.

Enough of trying to play smart! If you will follow God's rules and regulations for living, He can turn things around for your good! Regardless of the situation you may find yourself at present, that is not the end of the road for you. It is not final! God can always surprise you if you will surrender your total life and affairs to Him. He will always guide your steps in life and at the end, you will share testimonies to His glory. Moreover, do not walk alone. Two are better than one. Endeavour to seek for counsel on matters of concern. Do not bottle up issues in your heart. No life challenges can sink you! There is hope for you.

Encourage yourself in the Lord. Simply note that you are not finished yet when you are defeated. Do not give room to the devil. Also, fret not in your heart or worry. You are to take everything to God in prayers.

SPIRIT OF ENVY AND JEALOUSY

"For jealousy is the rage of a man: therefore he will not spare in the day of vengeance. He will not regard any ransom; neither will he rest content, though thou givest many gifts...Wrath is cruel, and anger is outrageous; but who is able to stand before envy?" (Proverbs 6:34-35; 27:4). Envy and jealousy are twin representations of pride and complex evils that must never be given a breathing space in the congregation of Christians. As Satan, who desired to be like the Most High God, envy means to desire something that someone else has by all means. It is numbered among the works of the flesh. The book of Job has this to say about it. "For wrath killeth the foolish man, and envy slayeth the silly one" (Job 5:2).

Envy is a human emotion and an act of covetousness to have for yourself what rightfully belongs to another person while jealousy is having a constant string of negative thoughts and words about other people. It is as strong and as poisonous as the venom of a snake. It diverts your attention to other people rather than focusing on God with absolute trust and contentment just like Cain, in Genesis 4:3-7, was jealous of his brother Abel, who received God's favour. Instead of him to seek God's face in repentance, he slew his brother and became the first murderer on the surface of the earth as recorded in the Bible.

Satan is the father of all murderers. On the contrary, God's jealousy symbolizes His affection towards us for our own good. It is in His nature of holiness with holy indignation to punish the offenders that transgress against His commandments as creatures. But God is not envious of our affections if we reverence and worship Him as the only living God. Envy is an open door to other wicked acts such as jealousy, hatred and murder. Envy is an offshoot of carnal comparison that breeds the wicked devices of Satan. Lack of contentment with what we have leads to carnal competition in relationships. It causes division, destructive gossip, hatred, resentment, cruelty, strife, depression, vengeful spirit and murder. Christians should watch their passions and be contented with what they have. We have to repent in any area we have gone astray, bind this murderous spirit and resist the devil continually with all vigilance and watchfulness. Moreover, we should pray with all supplications to uproot this work of the flesh and mortify it.

SPIRIT OF LUST AND IMMORALITY

In the New Testament of the Bible, the Greek word "porneia" is most often translated "sexual immorality." Also, it is translated as whoredom, lusting, fornication (premarital sexual relations), adultery, prostitution, homosexuality and bestiality. It is an involvement in sexual activities outside Biblical injunctions. The spirit behind it is the devil. "But I say unto you, that whosoever looketh on a woman to lust after her hath committed adultery with her already in his heart" (Matthew 5:28).

Immorality begins with a lustful eye set on the opposite sex. There is nothing wrong in seeing a beautiful or a handsome person because it is a natural phenomenon to see things and appreciate them. But looking lustfully and paying undue attention to what we see could be dangerous. The devil is a manipulator and can take advantage by sending a wrong signal into our hearts which, if wrongly processed, can lead to physical manifestation of fornication or adultery. The spirit of immorality begins and grows through lusting in the heart and once the heart is defiled, the devil has the legal right to manipulate it up until sin is committed.

Our eyes are the gateway to our heart, we must discipline our eyes on what we watch or see as Job did. "I made a covenant with mine eyes; why then should I think upon a maid?" (Job 31:1). Like Job, we can fill the heart through the eye-gate with the Word of God. The spirit of immorality doesn't happen suddenly. It is very subtle and grows into a foothold first; later, it becomes a demonic stronghold of obsession that graduates into sexual impurity and immorality. Demons always pay close attention to those who always lust in order to gain entrance into their lives. Satan continues to promote the activities of the kingdom of darkness through sexual immorality mostly caused by sensual and sexy dressings which attract demons that promote carnality and sexual perversion.

"Ye adulterers and adulteresses, know ye not that the friendship of the world is enmity with God? whosoever therefore will be a friend of the world is the enemy of God" (James 4:4). Some folks perform beauty or cosmetic surgeries to make them look extremely sexy beyond their natural outlook, going around with demonic dedicated cloths to hunt men (Romans 1:24-27). Similarly, the devil did not stop there; his target is to defile the church through carnality and sexual impurity (Revelation 2:14, 20-22).

Sex is holy when it involves a husband and his wife in marriage. It is God's mystery but remember that Satan is a counterfeit god with evil intentions to thwart God's purpose of sexual relationship in bringing intimacy between married couples. Sex makes a man and woman one flesh. It is an emotional or sexual bond (called soul tie) that promotes relationship (Genesis 2:25); but the type of sex that Satan offers is lust and immorality. This is an ungodly soul-tie that leads to bondage and damnation of soul! Be warned (1 Corinthians 7:1-7).

Satan continues to deceive and pollute the minds of many people today through pornography. This enslaves boys, girls, men and women by initiating them with the spirit of lust and immorality. Crimes of sexual abuse, rape and incest are linked to pornography. Sexual perversion, fornication and adultery are dividends of lust and immorality that lower the moral values of any society today.

Another level of sexual bondage comes from the use of sexual objects like sex toys, artificial breasts, bum, buttocks; and sex dolls. All are satanic deceptions that would damn souls in hell. "But the fearful, and unbelieving, and the abominable, and murderers, and whoremongers, and sorcerers, and idolaters, and all liars, shall have their part in the lake which burneth with fire and brimstone: which is the second death" (Revelation 21:8). Believers in Christ need to watch and guide against carnal appetite and inordinate affection that the devil is using to destroy many people these last days. The sin of lust and immorality has brought down more people than any other sin in the Bible. Thousands of the people of Israel died in the wilderness for engaging in immorality with Moabites. David, the greatest king of Israel, committed the sin of immorality with Bathsheba (Uriah's wife). Solomon's heart was turned away from God by his wives and concubines. Be warned!

SPIRIT OF INFIRMITY

The spirit of infirmity causes sicknesses by demonic activities and inflicts diseases through agents of Satan to cause weakness and disorder in the body. Satan means business in bringing many people into bondage and subjecting them to sicknesses and pains. Conversely, because of this purpose, God gave us His only begotten Son - Jesus Christ, to destroy every work of the devil in the lives of those who surrender their lives to Him today! "And, behold, there was a woman which had a spirit of infirmity eighteen years, and was bowed together, and could in no wise lift up herself. And when Jesus saw her, he called her to him, and said unto her, Woman, thou art loosed from thine infirmity ...How God anointed Jesus of Nazareth with the Holy Ghost and with power: who went about doing good, and healing all that were oppressed of the devil; for God was with him" (Luke 13:11-12; Acts 10:38).

Demonic spirits from Satan that were attached to the body of this woman caused ailments in her body. Such ailments will definitely defy treatment and medication. There is the deaf and dumb demonic spirit that causes mental illness and foaming in the mouth due to epilepsy just to destroy the lives of its victims (Mark 9:17-27). Demons cause a lot of diseases, sicknesses, suicides and disasters. They cause deformity (Luke 13:11-17), suffering, torture and torment (Matthew 15:22), insanity (Luke 8:26-35), dumbness (Matthew 9:32,33), personal injuries (Mark 9:18), perversion and deviation from revealed truth (1 Timothy 4:1-3), encouragement and promotion of idolatry (1 Corinthians 10:20, 21) and departure from the faith (1 Timothy 4:1; 2 Timothy 2:17, 18). Satan gained entrance through sin and attack people's bodies, thinking patterns and emotions with sicknesses and diseases.

Nevertheless, not all sicknesses are caused by demon. Some sicknesses come naturally as a result of breaking the rules of hygiene. Satan can entice and tempt us to sin or our emotions could be attacked to make us angry and lust on mundane things of this world which could entrap us if we yield to it. A person who contracted HIV/AIDS from the same sex or the opposite sex cannot say that he was attacked by the devil. In this case, his ailment comes from indulgence in the sinful habit of immorality.

Physical or natural ailments may come in form of pains, grief, sorrow, sickness, disease, infective agents, air pollution and natural disasters. Either demon-caused or nature-caused infirmities, Jesus has authority over all sicknesses and diseases. "Surely he hath borne our griefs, and carried our sorrows: yet we did esteem him stricken, smitten of God, and afflicted. But he was wounded for our transgressions, he was bruised for our iniquities: the chastisement of our peace was upon him; and with his stripes we are healed…Then he called his twelve disciples together, and gave them power and authority over all devils, and to cure diseases" (Isaiah 53:4-5; Luke 9:1).

There is power in the Blood, Word and Name of Jesus Christ! He has given us authority as well to cast out demons and heal all manner of sicknesses and diseases. Hence Christ expects us to exercise our authority in prayer as we pray for the sick by binding the devil and casting out the spirit of infirmity in Jesus' name and by pleading the blood of Jesus to destroy the root-cause of the infirmity and commanding healing in the mighty name of Jesus Christ.

ANTICHRIST SPIRIT

"Beloved, believe not every spirit, but try the spirits whether they are of God: because many false prophets are gone out into the world. Hereby know ye the Spirit of God: Every spirit that confesseth that Jesus Christ is come in the flesh is of God: And every spirit that confesseth not that Jesus Christ is come in the flesh is not of God: and this is that spirit of antichrist, whereof ye have heard that it should come; and even now already is it in the world" (1 John 4:1-3).

The above Scriptural verses confirm that the antichrist spirit is in the world today. It is the spirit of the end times controlling the demonic forces that operate as agents of Satan which opposes the truth about Christ and the works of salvation. It is a spirit assigned and empowered by Satan to deceive and pervert the way of righteousness with false signs and wonders all just to bring many people into greater bondage. Moreover, the antichrist will only show up after the rapture and specifically during the Great Tribulation as an object of worship who will open his mouth to utter blasphemous words against the God of Heaven and oppose all that is called God on earth. As the lawless man of sin and son of perdition, he would pervert the truth and prevent many souls from seeking the way of truth. He is a diabolical dictator that would rule and lead the whole world into total rebellion against God (2 Thessalonians 2:3-10).

But the Spirit of God is the Spirit truth that would guide all true believers into all truth to be able to discern all deceptive spirits known as antichrist spirits. They are at work against the Christian faith and the church at large with great delusion. Christians should never give up in the fight against the spirit that opposes Christ and the enemy of humanity!

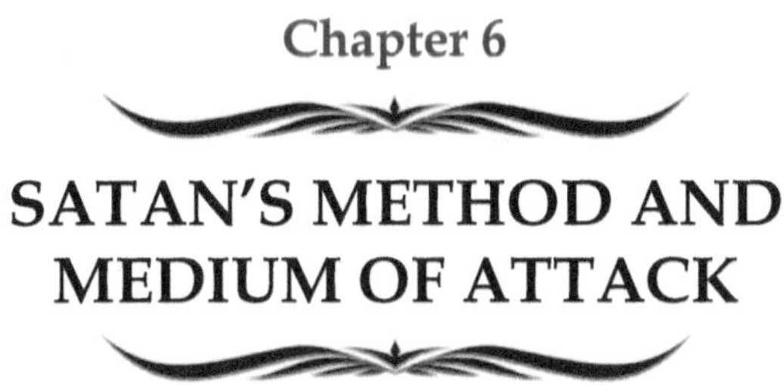

Satan is not omnipotent or omniscient and cannot work alone or be in every place at the same time because he is not omnipresent. He networks to carry out his wickedness using his agents - evil spirits, demons, unclean spirits, (Jude 6); principalities, powers, world rulers, spiritual wicked forces in high places (Ephesians 6:12). He also uses unbelievers - witches and wizards, familiar spirit (John 8:44) and occasionally, he uses unguarded Christians as temporary volunteer workers to accomplished evil purposes (Mark 8:31-32).

SATANIC MANIPULATION

Cambridge Advanced Learner's Dictionary described manipulation as "controlling someone or something to your own advantage, often unfairly of dishonestly." This is exactly what Satan does! He craftily influences people for his own advantage when all direct tactics fail. The purpose of Satan's manipulation is to paint sin in other colours, making it so attractive for us to commit against God.

In 2 Corinthians 11:14 and 1 Timothy 4:1-4, "And no marvel; for Satan himself is transformed into an angel of light ...Now the Spirit speaketh expressly, that in the latter times some shall depart from the faith, giving heed to seducing spirits, and doctrines of devils; Speaking lies in hypocrisy; having their conscience seared with a hot iron; Forbidding to marry, and commanding to abstain from meats, which God hath created to be received with thanksgiving of them which believe and know the truth."

Satan manipulated Eve in the Garden of Eden and caused her and Adam to sin against God with consequences of curse and death upon humanity. He did not stop there; he was the brain behind the evil and calamity of both Cain and Esau. It was the same old serpent that provoked David to number Israel, causing the death of seventy thousand men and bringing destruction upon Jerusalem (1 Chronicles 21:1, 14-15). Satan has always remained the author of confusion and evil. He put a lying spirit in the mouth of the old prophet to deceive the young prophet who was sent by God on a mission and made him disobey God (1 Kings 13:11-25). It was the same devil that tempted our Lord Jesus Christ and manipulated Peter to persuade Jesus against the purpose of God for the redemptive work on the cross at Calvary in order to hinder the salvation of humanity (Matthew 4:1-11; 16:21-23).

We thank God that Satan failed woefully and could not hinder the plan of God. In like manner, Satan is still working to frustrate the grace of God in our lives if he has a breathing space to manipulate and cause problem. "Lest Satan should get an advantage of us: for we are not ignorant of his devices" (2 Corinthians 2:11). Demonic manipulation against Christians may lead them to compromise, sell their birthright, backslide and sin. This calls for vigilance, self-examination, regular study of God's word and prayers.

MENTAL (MIND) ATTACKS

"And withal they learn to be idle, wandering about from house to house; and not only idle, but tattlers also and busybodies, speaking things which they ought not...Keep thy heart with all diligence; for out of it are the issues of life" (1 Timothy 5:13; Proverbs 4:23).

God warned us to keep our hearts from negative thoughts because the mind of man is the domain and first target of enemy attacks. The mind is the greatest focus of Satan's attacks in man's life where he can be in charge to establish his stronghold. He does this by throwing us off the center of God's will to distract us by negative thoughts and ideas that would render us ineffective in God's Kingdom. There is a battle going on within as Satan is trying to take control of your mind from time to time. The Bible declared that, "For as he thinketh in his heart, so is he: Eat and drink, saith he to thee; but his heart is not with thee" (Proverbs 23:7).

Satan wants you to think of fear, doubt, hatred, suspicious and evil so as to put you into bondage to his will. If he succeeds, he will be in control of your mind and build his stronghold there. Therefore, what you see, hear and meditate upon play a significant role in your mind and life. Satan is a liar and he will use lies, deception and false gossip about others to open up your mind to his attacks as a person.

In other words, gossiping unconstructively about others do you more harm than the person you are trying to castigate and destroy because Satan will first attack your mind this way and make you his instrument and victim. "These six things doth the LORD hate: yea, seven are an abomination unto him: A proud look, a lying tongue, and hands that shed innocent blood, An heart that deviseth wicked imaginations, feet that be swift in running to mischief, A false witness that speaketh lies, and he that soweth discord among brethren…An ungodly man diggeth up evil: and in his lips there is as a burning fire" (Proverbs 6:16-19; 16:27).

Through these vices, you become an instrument in the hands of Satan as he messes with your mind to suppress your mentality with negative thoughts about others to your own peril. Your belief in false assumptions and lies of the devil will lead you into wrong actions and reactions. In like manner, the enemy uses a cycle of our carnal thoughts in the subconscious mind to attack us. Our background from childhood, tradition and belief system form our thought pattern, and lifestyle. This carnal nature begins to develop in our subconscious with emotion and temperament. This is why we are getting attacks from this nature from time to time but God's purpose for us is good. "And the peace of God, which surpasses all comprehension, will guard your hearts and your minds in Christ Jesus" (Philippians 4:7).

Sinful thoughts come from a corrupt mind. The bad opinions that were programmed in you from birth as a result of ugly experiences such as abuse and molestation develop into character flaws that form untoward life patterns and practices. These become a habit that defiles us if we fail to renew our mind daily with God's Word. Romans 12:1-2 says, "I beseech you therefore, brethren, by the mercies of God, that ye present your bodies a living sacrifice, holy, acceptable unto God, which is your reasonable service. And be not conformed to this world: but be ye transformed by the renewing of your mind, that ye may prove what is that good, and acceptable, and perfect, will of God."

Another area of attack is through demonic thoughts. This type of thought process is oppressive and comes from Satan. It always comes with fear, worries and anxiety which arise from pessimism - a premonition that something evil will happen. Satan attacks our minds with worldly thoughts. This kind of thought makes you to love the things of the world at the detriment of your own soul. God knows that the devil can get us distracted and He warned: "Love not the world, neither the things that are in the world. If any man love the world, the love of the Father is not in him. For all that is in the world, the lust of the flesh, and the lust of the eyes, and the pride of life, is not of the Father, but is of the world. And the world passeth away, and the lust thereof: but he that doeth the will of God abideth forever" (1 John 2:15-17).

The devil uses the lust of eyes, the lust of flesh and the pride of life to draw us away from God and build his stronghold of worldliness in our live when we imitate the people of the world as he did to Demas (2 Timothy 4:10). But, "Now the just shall live by faith: but if any man draw back, my soul shall have no pleasure in him. But we are not of them who draw back unto perdition; but of them that believe to the saving of the soul" (Hebrews 10:38-39). My prayer is that we would not draw back and Satan will not get a hold of us in Jesus' name.

How then can you win and defeat the strongholds of Satan in your life? In 2 Corinthians 10:3-6, "For though we walk in the flesh, we do not war after the flesh: (For the weapons of our warfare are not carnal, but mighty through God to the pulling down of strong holds;) Casting down imaginations, and every high thing that exalteth itself against the knowledge of God, and bringing into captivity every thought to the obedience of Christ; And having in a readiness to revenge all disobedience, when your obedience is fulfilled."

The first thing you need to believe in your heart is that Satan and his evil forces have been defeated by Christ already on the Cross of Calvary as victory for all believers in Him. Satan is a defeated foe, so, we have nothing to fear anymore each time he tries to raise his ugly head. Secondly, you need to have faith in God and believe that Satan has been defeated for you. Claim the victory! Thirdly, you must identify the thought and nature of the strongholds. Fourthly, you have to confess it and repent for allowing the strongholds to build up and dominate your mind. Fifthly, ask God to sanctify your heart and cleanse you from inward pollution (Hebrews 10:10-25). Lastly, declare God's Word of truth always, renounce every negative thought and renew your mind daily with God's promises in all humility of heart (Romans 12:1-2; 1 Peter 5:6-7).

EVIL ALTARS AND DEDICATIONS

"For according to the number of thy cities were thy gods, O Judah; and according to the number of the streets of Jerusalem have ye set up altars to that shameful thing, even altars to burn incense unto Baal" (Jeremiah 11:13). This verse revealed the existence of evil altars. The direct messengers of Satan such as the principalities, powers and rulers of darkness are the authorities behind evil altars. It is a place, object or thing dedicated for spiritual sacrifice to Satan and his emissaries. An evil altar is a demonic dedicated place where agents of darkness do communicate with the spirit world to invoke demons for attacking their victims. At the evil altar, enchantments, divinations, sorceries and invocations are carried out by worshippers of Satan for demonic power and authority to wreak havoc or activate an evil agreement or create a relationship or contract with Satan for special assignments. Satan cannot give you free things without your paying very dearly for it because he has no free gifts! When he gives you a cap, it is to take your head in return!

An evil altar is a place of fellowship with evil cohorts and members of the kingdom of darkness. It is a demonic point of contact to steal, kill and destroy lives and properties. An evil altar is a place of evil attacks and operations where the progress of victims is impeded. It is a location where blessings are blocked or tied down, where destinies are destroyed and people's health are demonically attacked with infirmities that defy medication. There are many types of altars such as family altars, forest altars, marine altars, graveyard altars, terrestrial altars, road altars, pathway altars, astral altars and territorial altars. The myriads of problems in the lives of men had earlier been settled in any of these evil altars before their physical manifestations.

Take for instance, someone who experiences mysterious barrenness whose cause health professionals could not diagnose. It might be probably as a result of her womb being dedicated to the evil altar of barrenness. It might also be the product of unbroken curses as a result of past relationships and unbroken covenant with the devil. Since Satan rebelled against God, he has been trying to imitate everything about God. He knows the consequences of breaking a covenant and as a roaring lion, he uses this to afflict the generations of those who worship him if the covenant and agreement between them is broken.

Gideon broke free from the consequences of the evil altar of his father's house by destroying the altar of Baal and replacing it with a new altar that he built to the Lord God of Israel. "And it came to pass the same night, that the LORD said unto him, Take thy father's young bullock, even the second bullock of seven years old, and throw down the altar of Baal that thy father hath, and cut down the grove that is by it: And build an altar unto the LORD thy God upon the top of this rock, in the ordered place, and take the second bullock, and offer a burnt sacrifice with the wood of the grove which thou shalt cut down" (Judges 6:25-26).

Except such a person takes a drastic step like Gideon and genuinely repents of his sins by renouncing evil associations and surrendering all to the Lordship of Jesus Christ, the devil has the legal right to afflict him. Only Jesus Christ can save and deliver from the hands of Satan and his agents. In the Old Testament, Jacob, Joshua, Gideon and David, to mention but few of them, built altars unto the Lord (Genesis 35:7; Joshua 8:30; Judges 6:22-27; and 2 Samuel 24:25).

UNBROKEN CURSES

"As the bird by wandering, as the swallow by flying, so the curse causeless shall not come" (Proverbs 26:2). Concealed and undetected to unbroken curses are the source of many people today. Many are perishing because of ignorance and lack of knowledge of the fundamental source of their life troubles. In general terms, sinners are cursed already except they repent and accept Jesus as Lord and Saviour, before they can enjoy the provisions of God's blessings through the atoning blood of Jesus Christ that was shed on the cross of Calvary for the remission of sins. The book of Galatians 3:13-14 says, "Christ hath redeemed us from the curse of the law, being made a curse for us: for it is written, Cursed is every one that hangeth on a tree: That the blessing of Abraham might come on the Gentiles through Jesus Christ; that we might receive the promise of the Spirit through faith."

Salvation is the fundamental experience of God's grace, the greatest miracle that can ever happened to man in this world of sins. It is deliverance from curses and dominion over all forms of satanic harassment. At the same time, there are Christians who deliberately handle unholy things and break vows to God. This opens the door to bondage and satanic afflictions. "Cursed be he that doeth the work of the LORD deceitfully, and cursed be he that keepeth back his sword from blood...Shake thyself from the dust; arise, and sit down, O Jerusalem: loose thyself from the bands of thy neck,

O captive daughter of Zion… Depart ye, depart ye, go ye out from thence, touch no unclean thing; go ye out of the midst of her; be ye clean, that bear the vessels of the LORD" (Jeremiah 48:10; Isaiah 52:2, 11).

Unfortunately, many professed Christians are yet to discover the truth about the redemptive work of our Lord Jesus Christ. They professed to be Christians but do not understand the fundament principles of Christianity. There was a time that a friend's wife, in my country of birth, newly put to bed. She was not properly fed with good diet for the period of eight days after delivery. According to the custom and tradition of that family lineage, the woman must be restricted to certain kinds of poor quality food for the period of eight days because of a curse pronounced by a slave woman that was underfed and maltreated for eight days after delivery of her baby in their ancestral history.

As this woman was dying, she pronounced a curse on every woman in that family lineage. Many years after her demise and up until today, any woman who secretly eats good or delicious food before eight days will die mysteriously. Young women that newly put to bed were always found dead within the eight days of delivery until they consulted with the oracle in the family that revealed this fact. I did not know this before until I visited my wife to see her treated that way. As I could not hold my peace anymore, I decided to challenge my friend (a Christian though) on why he allowed his wife to be treated in a similar manner. My friend feared that his wife would die, so, he submitted to the family tradition. The Bible declared that, "The curse of the LORD is in the house of the wicked: but he blesseth the habitation of the just. Surely he scorneth the scorners: but he giveth grace unto the lowly" (Proverbs 3:33-34).

There are generational curses that abide upon families as a result of the wickedness, sins and idol worship of forefathers, while others are the architect of their own problems by their mischievous attitudes towards God and their fellow man. Mysterious battles and untold sufferings characterize the lifestyles of the people operating under curses and have affected many people, families, communities and nations. "And shed innocent blood, even the blood of their sons and of their daughters, whom they sacrificed unto the idols of Canaan: and the land was polluted with blood. Thus, were they defiled with their own works, and went a whoring with their own inventions. Therefore was the wrath of the LORD kindled against his people, insomuch that he abhorred his own inheritance" (Psalms 106:38-40).

Likewise, curses can come from God when men break His covenant (John 15:6; Exodus 20:4-6; Malachi 3:8-12). Curses can come from Satan and his agents when man breaks the edge of God's protection. This gives the devil a legal right to attack or curse (Ecclesiastes 10:8; 1 Peter 5:8-9). Lastly, curses can come from someone who has been wronged. Elisha cursed Gehazi (2 Kings 5:20-27), Jacob cursed Reuben (Genesis 49:3-4). In any situation of man's life, God is full of mercy and has made provision for all curses to be cancelled and broken through Jesus Christ. Genuine repentance from sin and idolatry, revoking the curses by the blood that Jesus Christ had shed on the cross and casting out the demons associated with the curse will bring deliverance in the name of Jesus. Besides, Christians have the authority to break generational curses and cast out demons in the name of Jesus (Mark 16:17-18; Luke 10:17-19).

Chains, yokes and spells shall be broken by the blood and by the mighty name of Jesus Christ through Whom Christians are translated from generational curses to generational blessings (Galatians 3:13-14). Hence a life of obedience to God's word and faithfulness will enable us enjoy the provision of God's blessings. It is also good to know that the devil cannot change the promises of God or curse any child of God. There are blessings for the righteous to enjoy in Christ Jesus and for all his seeds after him in their generations. Therefore, the choice is yours to choose blessings rather than curses today. "And it shall come to pass, when all these things are come upon thee, the blessing and the curse, which I have set before thee, and thou shalt call them to mind among all the nations, whither the LORD thy God hath driven thee...I call heaven and earth to record this day against you, that I have set before you life and death, blessing and cursing: therefore choose life, that both thou and thy seed may live" (Deuteronomy 30:1, 19).

The problems of many people today can be traced to their foundations as many would have been cursed by the agent of Satan before they were born or after birth. Some curses are generational and need to be completely broken for generational blessings to manifest from God. The case of Jabez is a typical example of a curse at birth. "And Jabez was more honourable than his brethren: and his mother called his name Jabez, saying, Because I bare him with sorrow. And Jabez called on the God of Israel, saying, Oh that thou wouldest bless me indeed, and enlarge my coast, and that thine hand might be with me, and that thou wouldest keep me from evil, that it may not grieve me! And God granted him that which he requested" (1 Chronicles 4: 9-10).

Jabez discovered that his problem was from the foundation. This knowledge helped him to turn to the God of Israel in prayer for deliverance and divine solution. Here, we see that no pastor or prophet was involved except the God of Israel and the curse was broken! Some children are placed under curses unknown to them during child dedication, most especially, when initiated with demonic names related to family idols and the sacrifice offered to ancestral spirits by the elders. In this situation, Jesus Christ remains the only solution when the foundation is destroyed (Psalms 11:3). Such people need to turn to Calvary where Jesus bled and died to pay the price of redemption that broke all curses. Also, it is good to know that there are patterns of good or bad traits in every family bloodline. Believers are admonished to research and know the background of their family genealogy. This knowledge will help us to discover whether our forefathers had covenanted with the devil on a particular matter that could give the devil a legal right to torment or hinder blessings. Just like Daniel, who had knowledge of the sins of his forefathers and confessed them to God (Daniel 9:1-19), this awareness will give such believers an opportunity to confess every sin and break evil patterns through the name of Jesus.

DEMONIC MONITORING SPIES

"The thief cometh not, but for to steal, and to kill, and to destroy: I am come that they might have life, and that they might have it more abundantly...Be sober, be vigilant; because your adversary the devil, as a roaring lion, walketh about, seeking whom he may devour" (John 10:10; 1 Peter 5:8). Monitoring spies of Satan are demonic forces assigned from the kingdom of darkness to steal blessings, cashier destinies, kill personal dreams, thwart aspirations and destroy lives. There are many virtues that this enemy has stolen and kept in the demonic strong room or demonic bank. In most cases, the victims are often attacked in their dreams by snakes, tigers, lions, cats, dogs, black birds, crows or by having sex in the dream. Through the activities of these messengers of darkness, many have witnessed series of disappointments, untold hardships, heartbreaks, delay to answered prayers - all to frustrate them in life. Monitoring spies or spirits are witchcraft weapons often used to harass prospects, torment victims and frustrate their Christian faith. Again, monitoring spies are used as a weapon to hinder or delay progress, marriages, child bearing, promotion at work and opportunities.

Many years ago, at my country of birth, two elderly men were discussing about one of the family members that travelled far away from the homeland. For a long time, they did not hear from him. However, they consulted their oracle and poured water to fill a basin and inquired about his wellbeing. Through their sorcery and divination, they were able to see the video of this man and his family abroad. They saw the wife and the two children sitting on the dining chair according to them. They pressed further to ask the particular time he would visit home and they got to know the time he planned to visit his homeland through their monitoring sprit and divination. The man came visiting at the exact time their oracle told them.

The demonic world is real, but many are ignorant or in denial of this salient truth. But for Christians, "The angel of the Lord encampeth round about them that fear him, and delivereth them" (Psalms 34:7). God will surely answer us if we experience this type of battle. God is ever faithful to deliver His children from the hands of the wicked one. We must pray that God should break generational tides and curses that bind us to family evil patterns. We have to break and destroy their demonic mirrors, evil altars, gadgets, demonic communication networks, all remote control mechanisms and devices used to monitor us. Let us call down God's fire to destroy them totally.

DEMONIC COBWEBS ATTACK

"None calleth for justice, nor any pleadeth for truth: they trust in vanity, and speak lies; they conceive mischief, and bring forth iniquity. They hatch cockatrice' eggs, and weave the spider's web: he that eateth of their eggs dieth, and that which is crushed breaketh out into a viper. Their webs shall not become garments, neither shall they cover themselves with their works: their works are works of iniquity, and the act of violence is in their hands. Their feet run to evil, and they make haste to shed innocent blood: their thoughts are thoughts of iniquity; wasting and destruction are in their paths. The way of peace they know not; and there is no judgment in their goings: they have made them crooked paths: whosoever goeth therein shall not know peace" (Isaiah 59:4-8).

Demonic cobweb attacks are parts of the strategies of the enemies to render their victims, things and places devastated and desolate. The target of the enemy is to trap the blessings coming to you and block your advancement in life. In the natural realm, cobweb is the spider's web which it uses to trap other insects for foods. So also, the enemies of progress use it to trap people's destiny, paralyze their dream and cause blockages to their progress.

For instance, whenever you are going along in an open place or on the main road and you physically feel a sign of webs covering your forehead or face, sometimes, it is a sign of demonic webs or an attack from the enemy. This is common in African countries, but for believers in Christ, this is what God is saying, "Thus saith the LORD to his anointed, to Cyrus, whose right hand I have holden, to subdue nations before him; and I will loose the loins of kings, to open before him the two leaved gates; and the gates shall not be shut; I will go before thee, and make the crooked places straight: I will break in pieces the gates of brass, and cut in sunder the bars of iron: And I will give thee the treasures of darkness, and hidden riches of secret places, that thou mayest know that I, the LORD, which call thee by thy name, am the God of Israel" (Isaiah 45:1-3).

All demonic blockages, barriers and circle of limitations shall be broken in pieces by the God of our salvation through prayers of faith by pleading the blood of Jesus upon your life and all things that pertain to you. When you ask the fire of God to destroy all demonic blockages, obstacles and barriers in your paths and ways, it shall be so done in Jesus' name.

Chapter 7

WITCHCRAFT ACTIVITIES

The origin of witchcraft has been since the fall of man in the Garden of Eden. Its activities originated from Satan. Similar to witchcraft practices are voodoo, wicca, black magic, sorcery and wizardry. Consequent upon the Fall, man lost God and settled for Satan's cheap alternative. As he persistently desired for fellowship with the supernatural, he started a misguided adventure into the depth of satanic activities and practices. The power of witchcraft and deadly operations are the manifestations of satanic forces to unleash wickedness and destruction in human's life.

God's stand against witchcraft activities still holds today for us to obey. "There shall not be found among you any one that maketh his son or his daughter to pass through the fire, or that useth divination, or an observer of times, or an enchanter, or a witch. Or a charmer, or a consulter with familiar spirits, or a wizard, or a necromancer. For all that do these things are an abomination unto the Lord: and because of these abominations the Lord thy God doth drive them out from before thee" (Deuteronomy 18:10-12).

God always has controversy with evil men who practice witchcraft and has commanded His people to separate from all forms of satanic activities and practices. In the Old

Testament, there is a death penalty for those who engaged in the evil act of witchcraft as He commanded, "Thou shalt not suffer a witch to live" (Exodus 22:18).. But the grace of God rules this age of the New Testament with provision of forgiveness for all who truly repent. This simply means that His judgement awaits all who dishonour God's warning against the practice of witchcraft. So then, whether it is White Witch, Red Witch or Black Witch, colour does not baptize or sanctify witchcraft. They are all absolutely satanic!

THE PRACTICE OF WITCHCRAFT

"Now the works of the flesh are manifest, which are these; Adultery, fornication, uncleanness, lasciviousness, Idolatry, WITCHCRAFT, hatred, variance, emulations, wrath, strife, seditions, heresies, Envyings, murders, drunkenness, revellings, and such like: of the which I tell you before, as I have also told you in time past, that they which do such things shall not inherit the kingdom of God" (Galatians 5:19-21). Witchcraft is among the works of the flesh that cause all sorts of injury to humans and to things or by casting hexes to inflict misfortune on others. The purpose of the devil and witchcraft attack is to rob God's people of God's glory and blessings. Anyone that practices any of above-listed works of flesh will end up in the lake of fire with Satan who gave him the evil ability to do so. Witchcraft attack starts from the heart through unforgiveness, bitterness, anger, envy, hatred and murder. These stages are the works of flesh. It is unforgiveness that degenerates to murder which prompts someone to consult mediums and shrines in other to destroy fellow human beings.

Other people's cravings for power, protection and authority have lured them into becoming white-witch agents of Satan and his captives. They are baited into witchcraft by their lust for power, popularity, prosperity, solution to the problems in the family and protection. By so doing, they willingly surrender their souls to the devil and get initiated into the kingdom of darkness. However, there are the ignorant captives known as blind witches who are initiated into the occultic world through unsolicited contact with agents of Satan, while others were dedicated by their parents through idol worship or food dedicated to idols.

Witchcraft operations are divers and subtle. The tools used are confusion, control, domination, manipulation, accusation, intimidation, attack, condemnation and draining the victims to total destruction. The witch manipulates the will of someone to dominate them and take absolute control of their lives as Eve was manipulated by Satan against God's will in the Garden of Eden. "Now the serpent was more subtle than any beast of the field which the Lord God had made. And he said unto the woman, Yea, hath God said, Ye shall not eat of every tree of the garden?" (Genesis 3:1).

Satan's manipulation perverted the original way of mankind. Telling lies in a diplomatic way to cause confusion, division, misunderstanding is the lifestyle of those who practice witchcraft. Likewise, Balak requested Prophet Balaam to curse the children of Israel in order to ensure that the nation's destiny is derailed and perverted from the will of God (Numbers 22:6, 22). Witchcraft operations and manifestations are always to find ways of imposing their will on their victims in all situations. Nevertheless, the promises of God are sure for those who will follow through and refuse to listen to the voice of strangers. Witchcraft attacks will constantly make you to feel guilty in all circumstances even when you are innocent.

The opportunity to prove your point when in disagreement with them would be disallowed. Rather, you would be left alone with hazy and clouded state of confused mind. Prophet Elijah had a similar experience with Jezebel, the wife of Ahab. "And Ahab told Jezebel all that Elijah had done, and withal how he had slain all the prophets with the sword. Then Jezebel sent a messenger unto Elijah, saying, So let the gods do to me, and more also, if I make not thy life as the life of one of them by tomorrow about this time. And when he saw that, he arose, and went for his life, and came to Beersheba, which belongeth to Judah, and left his servant there. But he himself went a day's journey into the wilderness, and came and sat down under a juniper tree: and he requested for himself that he might die; and said, It is enough; now, O Lord, take away my life; for I am not better than my fathers" (1 Kings 19:1-4). Witchcraft attack frustrated the prophet of holiness, who was zealous for the work of God, to the point that he was discouraged and prayed that God should take his life.

Another area of attack is bewitchment – the person is subjected to confusion of mind that he would not be able to discern or see beyond his nose through spell (incantation or spoken word for magical result). His life has been subjected and caged under the influence of demonic control and manipulation that could derail him from the good path. Witchcraft attack is extremely evil, it can cause mysterious accidents, sicknesses, barrenness, afflictions, loss of job and damaged reputations. Even a whole church can be bewitched.

In the case of the Galatian church, they were bewitched to believe the lies of the devil. Hence Apostle Paul came to them with a sharp rebuke to open their eyes. "O foolish Galatians, who hath bewitched you, that ye should not obey the truth, before whose eyes Jesus Christ hath been evidently set forth, crucified among you? This only would I learn of you, Received ye the Spirit by the works of the law, or by the hearing of faith? Are ye so foolish? having begun in the Spirit, are ye now made perfect by the flesh?... But there was a certain man, called Simon, which beforetime in the same city used sorcery, and bewitched the people of Samaria, giving out that himself was some great one: To whom they all gave heed, from the least to the greatest, saying, This man is the great power of God. And to him they had regard, because that of long time he had bewitched them with sorceries" (Galatians 3:1-3; Acts 8:9-11).

The work of the flesh began to manifest again in their Christian lives. We still need the likes of Apostle Paul today who would confront Simeon and Elymas the sorcerers on the pulpits where they are deceiving the people of God.

Ministers such as Paul will not spare the rod of correction in the midst of the congregation.

FAMILIAR SPIRIT

"Regard not them that have familiar spirits, neither seek after wizards, to be defiled by them: I am the LORD your God" (Leviticus 19:31). Moral laws of God remain in force in both the Old and New Testaments. Familiar spirit is a demonic spirit sent by the devil with access to the family history, trait and lifestyle. Family members get initiated and invited by the family elders through ancestral spirits to govern the family. Sometimes, it is called household repository and through this medium, information about the family or an individual can be made known by conjuring this demon to release the information he has stored to be used for attacking the victims.

Familiar spirits are responsible for mysterious problems that are genealogical and generational in nature within the family blood line which could be difficult for health professionals to diagnose. If you notice untimely deaths in the family, there are always spirits that would pass it to new generations to inherit as spirits don't die. The same captivity would be passing from generation to generation with recurrent sickness, oppression, barrenness and poverty as family stigmas and patterns. Witches and wizards always make use of the services of familiar spirits to find out information and facts that are needful for them to carry out their deadly operations.

Another way familiar spirits operate is explicit in what happened when King Saul sought the woman with a familiar spirit in Endor to give him information about Prophet Samuel who was resting in the bosom of the Lord (1 Samuel 28:6-20). Satan is a manipulator, deceiver and an impersonator. He manipulated things to satisfy the curiosity and appetite of Saul for Samuel. Job 7:9 says, "As the cloud is consumed and vanisheth away: so he that goeth down to the grave shall come up no more." Therefore, God could not give access to the devil to communicate with Samuel in Heaven because He abhorred necromancy and cannot contradict His Word which He exalteth above His name.

Likewise, many people are in bondage due to the manipulation of familiar spirits today because of their curiosity to know what the future holds for them. In their search for knowledge and prophecy, they get caught up in satanic webs of false prophets and their prophecies. "For such are false apostles, deceitful workers, transforming themselves into the apostles of Christ. And no marvel; for Satan himself is transformed into an angel of light. Therefore, it is no great thing if his ministers also be transformed as the ministers of righteousness; whose end shall be according to their works" (2 Corinthians 11:13-15).

Christians are warned to stay away from familiar spirits and admonished to "look unto Jesus, the author and the finisher of our faith..." Repent where necessary and renounce the ancestral monitoring spirit. This is very important because consultation with familiar spirits and agents of Satan attract

God's punishment as it happened to Saul. "So, Saul died for his transgression which he committed against the LORD, even against the word of the LORD, which he kept not, and also for asking counsel of one that had a familiar spirit, to enquire of it" (1 Chronicles 10:13).

BAITS TO DEMONIC POSSESSION AND PRACTICES

Satan is cunning and subtle. Most times, he does not appear in black or as an ugly and a fearful-looking person, but as a handsome, glamorous angel. "Lest Satan should get an advantage of us: for we are not ignorant of his devices... But I fear, lest by any means, as the serpent beguiled Eve through his subtitle, so your minds should be corrupted from the simplicity that is in Christ" (2 Corinthians 2:11; 11:3).

The devil operates in disguise; for he knows no sane person would wish to let him in if they know his identity. Knowing that many will not yield to the common and direct method of initiation into occultism, the devil employs a more subtle manner by appealing to the mind and desires of men to draw them into his net of oppression which usually develops into obsession; and if care is not taken, it becomes a case of possession. Demonic possession and practices usually begin unnoticed. Satan sends in the invitation baits to unsuspecting people. The people accept and the demons come in freely. By the time the victim became conscious of the presence of demons in their lives, the damage has been done already.

This is the reason the Lord warned His people to avoid witchcraft and occultism (Deuteronomy 18:9-12). This was the practice of heathen nations that do not know and serve the living God. In Egypt, when God wrought miracles through the hand of Moses, the Egyptians employed their demonic practices to replicate the miracles (Exodus 7:11, 12, 20-22). Manasseh engaged in demonic practices to the point that he provoked the Lord to anger (2 Chronicles 33:1-7).

Other demonic activities and possession in Bible days and today include:

Saul's consultation with the witch of Endor (1 Samuel 28:7-8).

- Ahab's worship of Baal (1 Kings 16:30-33).
- The maid with the spirit of divination (Acts 16:16).
- False religious practices: Star gazing, palm reading, seeking information from horoscope or psychic prophets (Deuteronomy 18:10-11).
- Rituals, burning of incense or candles, among others. (Ezekiel 8:11).
- Initiating others into demonism (Revelation 2:20; 2 Chronicles 33:6a).

Bait is an enticement to move from truth to falsehood: It is an allurement to leave safety and move into danger. The fish is lured from its peaceful abode into the entanglement of the fisher's net with bait. Similarly, the unguarded believer is tricked out of peace, joy, good health and divine favour with various kinds of baits. The devil has many baits at his disposal with which he entangles people and places them under demons' control. They include:

Food: Careless eaters pick up demons too soon. Food offered unto idols may open one up to demons or lead to initiation (1 Corinthians 10:19-21).

Necromancy: Contacting and contracting the dead (Deuteronomy 18:10-11).

False prophets and religions: Any religion that is not founded on Christ or one that is syncretic in nature is of the devil. Followers of such religion open themselves up to demon-possession. No doubt, those who worship angels, practice spiritism or engage in occultic services are fraternizing with demons (Mark 13:22).

Occultic music, dance and games: This include rap, pop, rock, demonic toys and games (Exodus 32:19; Mark 6:22; Philippians 4:8).

Occult Literature: Reading questionable, unscriptural and heretical books and magazines that do not edify the soul of man towards God (Acts 19:19).

Demo-induced fruit of the womb: Wrong search for children, secret knowledge or power through consultations with false prophets and fetish priests (Isaiah 8:19).

Desperate evil sacrifices: A desperate search for position, power, honour, fame, wealth, progress and promotion without caution, sometimes, leads the desperado into shedding blood through human sacrifice rituals.

There is the possibility of freedom for the victims of demonic operations. The Lord says, "Shall the prey be taken from the mighty, or the lawful captive delivered? But thus saith the LORD, Even the captives of the mighty shall be taken away, and the prey of the terrible shall be delivered: for I will contend with him that contendeth with thee, and I will save thy children" (Isaiah 49:24-25). The lawful captives shall be delivered if they turn to the Lord today because God has made provision for it (1 John 3:4, 8). The willing captive can be delivered, but:

There must be confession, repentance, revocation and renunciation of all evil activities, involvement in demonic practices and satanic covenants with occultic associations.

Captives must willingly accept Christ as personal Lord and Saviour. To remain demon-free, please, do the following:

- Confess all your sins to be forgiven (1 John 1:8-9).

- Renounce all sins and forsake them (Proverbs 28:13).

- Believe in Christ's death and atonement through His blood for your ransom and deliverance (Acts 16:30-31).

- Avoid sin like a plague (John 5:14).

- Destroy all properties of the devil. "And many that believed came, and confessed, and shewed their deeds. Many of them also which used curious arts brought their books together, and burned them before all men: and they counted the price of them, and found it fifty thousand pieces of silver (Acts 19:18-19).

- Consecrate your body unto the Lord and renew your mind daily with the Word of God (Romans 12:1-2).

- Cleave unto Christ through regular communion (Job 22:21; Psalms 5:3; 1 Chronicles 16:11).

- Fellowship regularly with God's people, study God's word daily and grow your faith (Hebrews 10:25; Joshua 1:8; 2 Timothy 2:15; Romans 10:17).

- Pray and watch, resisting every move of the devil to bring you down. (Matthew 26:41; 1 Peter 5:8-9).

- Avoid being unequally yoked (2 Corinthians 6:14-17).

- Keep yourself pure and abide in Christ to maintain your deliverance by living a life of holiness (1 John 5:18; John 15:1-7).

- Have a positive confession and exercise the believer's authority daily (Luke 10:19).

- Besides, be vigilant (1 Peter 5:8; Job 1:7; Matthew 26:41) Satan walks to and fro looking for whom he will devour. Always watch and be at alert! He is your arch enemy. Temptations and enticement are the baits he uses. Understand that Satan can tempt you with anything and can use anyone too. Do not rest not on your oars, but watch unto prayers (Matthew 13:33-37).

- Don't give room to the devil or else he will rubbish your testimony. Always resist him in the Name of Jesus! Yield not to the tempter. Ask for divine connection. Pray for divine assistance! Remember, God is able! The more the time you invest with Christ, the less stress you will experience.

Do these things because prevention is better and cheaper than cure.

Chapter 8

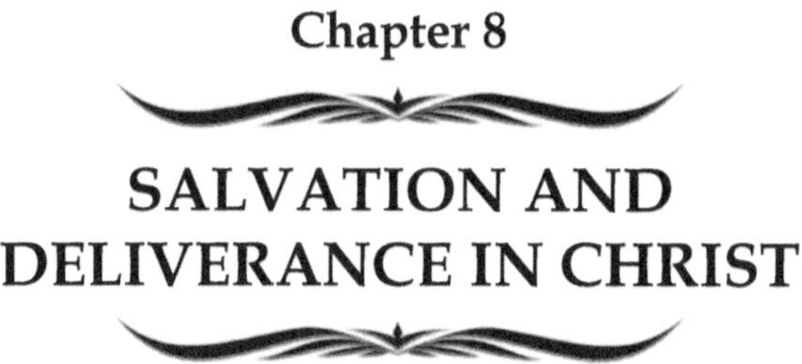

SALVATION AND DELIVERANCE IN CHRIST

"And almost all things are by the law purged with blood; and without shedding of blood is no remission…Then spake Jesus again unto them, saying, I am the light of the world: he that followeth me shall not walk in darkness, but shall have the light of life" (Hebrews 9:22; John 8:12).

Human beings are born sinners. We are born with the gene of sin inherited from Adam. No one is born free of this gene (or trait). Therefore, a natural human being cannot do but sin. No matter how hard a man tries, he cannot free himself from the inherited, hereditary bondage. We cannot get rid of our sin nature by our own efforts. Sin and Satan had plunged this old world into darkness, but Christ came as the Light of the world. For this reason, God took up the task of saving man, He offered His son, Jesus Christ, to shed His blood for the remission of all sins and die in our place.

The penalty for our sins has been paid through the blood Jesus shed for us on the cross of Calvary. Jesus is the universal Saviour having paid the full price of man's salvation in a vicarious capacity. Yet, you will not be saved if you don't believe in what Jesus did for your salvation and accept Him as Lord and Saviour.

The blood of Jesus does not only remove the guilt of sin but all associated problems as you plead it upon your life. It has the power to solve both spiritual and physical problems. His blood gives strength over sin, sickness and Satan. It is therefore necessary for man to seek the way of peace and reconciliation through the blood of Jesus Christ. Through faith in His blood, we have boldness and access with confidence to the throne of God to receive mercy at the time of need (Ephesians 3:12) and by His blood, we become joint heirs with our Lord Jesus. In addition, we can discover and operate the power for divine healing and health through the blood of Jesus (Isaiah 53:5).

"But what saith it? The word is nigh thee, even in thy mouth, and in thy heart: that is, the word of faith, which we preach; That if thou shalt confess with thy mouth the Lord Jesus, and shalt believe in thine heart that God hath raised him from the dead, thou shalt be saved. For with the heart man believeth unto righteousness; and with the mouth confession is made unto salvation. For the Scripture saith, Whosoever believeth on him shall not be ashamed. For there is no difference between the Jew and the Greek: for the same Lord over all is rich unto all that call upon him. For whosoever shall call upon the name of the Lord shall be saved" (Romans 10:8-13).

Again, you must acknowledge your sins by confessing them in prayer. Then, you must repent all sins and begin to live holily. All the works of darkness disappears from our lives as the light of Christ shines in and through us. Immorality, idol worship, magic, witchcraft, occultism, reveling, drunkenness and other sinful habits disappear from our lives as the light of Christ shines in and through us. Surely, God knows what you are passing through and He will see you through if you follow the blueprints of Salvation. This opens the door to the throne of grace to seek help in times of need and talk to God as your Father.

God also feels and knows every pain in your heart. Whatever the challenge, He knows and will see you through! Problems and difficulties are not difficult for Him to solve and resolve. Take the challenge or problem to Him in prayer. Talk to Him like a child to his father and let Him know everything that bothers your heart. Cast those burdens upon Him. Many are the afflictions of the righteous but the Lord delivers him from them all! Your case will not be different, but first search your heart and life. Jesus' love for humanity is unsurpassed. He shed His blood and became a sacrificial Lamb! All power in heaven and earth is under His control and authority. What a trust you need to have in such a wonderful Lord! There is nothing He cannot do for you - the man of Calvary indeed! Understand that for your sake, He left His glory in Heaven to resolve all issues for you!

Are you experiencing the pains of disappointment? Turn your eyes to Him in desperation. He would not turn you away unattended! Receive Him today and renew your consecration to Him! Make a firm decision to follow His dictates always. You need to appreciate the wonders of the cross as made available by the Lord of lords and the King of kings.

No one else can help you like Him. Draw closer to Him. Make sure nothing displeases Him in your life. If there is any infraction, ask for His pardon and forgiveness and put your trust and confidence in Him for solution and positive answers. Remember, God is greater than whatever you might be passing through. I am sure He will be merciful unto you if you call upon Him genuinely from your heart. The Lord Jesus ever cares – that I know!

GRACE, FORGIVENESS AND INWARD PURITY

"For the grace of God that bringeth salvation hath appeared to all men, Teaching us that, denying ungodliness and worldly lusts, we should live soberly, righteously, and godly, in this present world; Looking for that blessed hope, and the glorious appearing of the great God and our Saviour Jesus Christ; Who gave himself for us, that he might redeem us from all iniquity, and purify unto himself a peculiar people, zealous of good works…That he would grant unto us, that we being delivered out of the hand of our enemies might serve him without fear, In holiness and righteousness before him, all the days of our life" (Titus 2:11-14; Luke 1:74-75).

Salvation is entirely by grace; and grace has the potential to transform the most wretched sinner into a saint. Grace enables us to forgive our offenders and to desire the fullness of Christ so that the old nature may entirely give way to the new creature in Christ Jesus. We have no righteousness or good work that merits the favour of God; rather it is grace alone that brings the greatest miracle of salvation that man can ever received on earth. "For God so loved the world, that he gave his only begotten Son, that whosoever believeth in him should not perish, but have everlasting life" (John 3:16). God loves us, but he hates our sins. His love towards us compelled Him to send his only begotten Son to die for us on the cross of Calvary. Hence the only way to show our appreciation unto God for His gift of salvation is to give ourselves unto Him in absolute surrender.

Jesus has paid the full price for our redemption and we need to appropriate the sacrifice into our lives for we are saved by grace through faith in the finished work of Christ at Calvary. "Being justified freely by his grace through the redemption that is in Christ Jesus" (Romans 3:24). When grace is allowed to grow in us, it will make our lives beautiful before God and man. It also produces in us such purity of life that pleases God. Grace enables us to overcome all the ups and downs of life and still keeps us true to our calling as children of God. However, the grace of God can be lost when we try to pattern and live our lives the way we pleases. God has no desire in those who draw back (Hebrews 10:38). Furthermore, God expects that, since we are forgiven our numerous sins, we should be at peace with our fellowmen.

Forgiveness is easy when Jesus Christ has been enthroned in the heart through repentance and when there is willingness to obey Christ's command. Show me a man who forgives his neighbours easily and I will show you a man who has a personal encounter of genuine salvation with Jesus. Examples abound in the Scriptures of those that forgave freely and God took cognizance of their actions. Joseph forgave his brothers (Genesis 45:5-15; 50:19-21). David forgave Saul (1 Samuel 24:1-22; 2 Samuel 9:1-13). Jesus forgave those who crucified Him (Luke 23:34). Stephen forgave those who stoned him to death (Acts 7:54-60).

The rule of revenge is commonly practiced in our communities today to the point that people hunt one another with guns, charms and witchcraft attacks; but true Christians are governed by the Spirit of the living God. Through the grace upon us, we can easily forgive those who offend us. Forgiving others is the demonstration of God's grace and of the blessings that God bestows upon those who have given their lives to Jesus Christ in genuine repentance and accepting Him as Lord and personal Saviour.

"...if ye forgive men their trespasses, your heavenly Father will also forgive you: But if ye forgive not men their trespasses, neither will your Father forgive your trespasses (Matthew 6:14-15). Harbouring animosity, hatred and vengeful spirit is the work of the flesh and the very nature of Satan. You are also hurting yourself if you refuse to let go and let God rule in your life and situations. It is possible for us to say we have forgiven someone but still harbour grudges over the offence. This is why inner freedom becomes necessary.

There is an outward as well as an inward freedom. Once you find it difficult to forgive others and you hold them captive in your heart, it is a sign of inward depravity and you too are not free from the root of bitterness, grudge and animosity in the heart. At salvation, the shoots and roots of sin are destroyed in our spirit, but the nature of sins which remains in our body must be ruled by the Holy Spirit in us before we can be fit for Heaven at Christ's second coming. At salvation, it is our spirit that gets saved and not our body. The flesh can never be born again! That is why we must rule the flesh always by the Spirit to remain saved!

The fruit of the Spirit which is expected to be manifested at salvation is deepened when the inward depravity is dealt with. "But the fruit of the Spirit is love, joy, peace, longsuffering, gentleness, goodness, faith, Meekness, temperance: against such there is no law. And they that are Christ's have crucified the flesh with the affections and lusts" (Galatians 5:22-24). The disciples of Jesus were born again and were following the Lord Jesus, but the Bible recorded the evidences of position-seeking, bigotry, inconsiderate action and indignation in them (Mark 9:33-35: Matthew 26:6-13; Luke 9:51-56; Psalms 51:5).

There was need for freedom from moral corruption and pollution if they were to be set apart for sacred use. Hence Jesus prayed for the disciples before leaving them because the evidences of the nature of Adam were still in them. He prayed for their sanctification and for those who would believe in Him through the gospel message, thus: "Sanctify them through thy truth: thy word is truth. As thou hast sent me into the world, even so have I also sent them into the world. And for their sakes I sanctify myself, that they also might be sanctified through the truth. Neither pray I for these alone, but for them also which shall believe on me through their word" (John 17:17-20).

When our Lord Jesus Christ said, "…I sanctify myself, that they also might be sanctified…," here, the word 'sanctify' does not mean 'purify' but 'set apart' or 'consecrate' because Jesus has no sin and could never have prayed for His own cleansing or forgiveness. However, He prayed for His disciples' total consecration to God's service in all purity and this also applies to every believer today. Romans 12:1-3 captures it clearly, "I beseech you therefore, brethren, by the mercies of God, that ye present your bodies a living sacrifice, holy, acceptable unto God, which is your reasonable service." So, sanctification is not just a one-time experience or the product of self-struggle but of entirely surrendering ourselves to the Lord continually and refusing to yield to temptation at all times.

"And the Word was made flesh, and dwelt among us, (and we beheld his glory, the glory as of the only begotten of the Father,) full of grace and truth. John bare witness of him, and cried, saying, this was he of whom I spake, He that cometh after me is preferred before me: for he was before me. And of his fullness have all we received, and grace for grace. For the law was given by Moses, but grace and truth came by Jesus Christ. …But grow in grace, and in the knowledge of our

Lord and Saviour Jesus Christ. To him be glory both now and forever. Amen" (John 1:14-17; 2 Peters 3:18).

God always gives grace to the humble as it is only grace that can accomplish purity in any willing heart. God is in the business of uprooting inward depravity that harbours every work of the flesh if we allow Him. More grace will abound for you in Jesus' Name. On daily basis, may grace find you and abide with you. Nothing will stifle or limit grace in your life. Day by day, grace will be multiplied in your life. Always desire to grow in grace and in the knowledge of Christ. Yes, amazing, matchless, marvelous and wonderful grace are your portion in Jesus' Name.

Deepening your relationship with God is what you must pursue and ever drawing closer to Him in penitence and clean hands. Come to Jesus with humility and lowliness of heart. Engage in reading His Word, meditate on what you have read and build on your most holy faith, praying in the Holy Ghost. Ensure that His will is number one on your doing list. Rely and repose your hope and confidence in Him. This is what you need for this month and the rest of the year. May the Lord help you to keep to them.

Meditation is missing in many Christian's devotional life! After reading the Bible, there is need to ruminate on it and deeply digest what have read. Reading the Bible without meditation is not a complete devotional lifestyle. It is like doing only a part-time spiritual exercise. Create time for effective meditation daily. It will help you to have an in-depth understanding of the Word of God that you have read for practical application! How is your meditation life?

If you have been missing it, you have been missing a great spiritual resource that can translate you into a spiritual giant and general! Meditating on the Word of God will give you the strength to face each day's challenges successfully. Arising in the morning to seek the face of the Lord will help build your spiritual muscles and strength greatly. Yes, as you do so, it will make your soul to be satisfied with marrow and fatness day by day.

Thereafter, you need to maintain a good walk with God in purity of heart. Obey His commandments and truths implicitly. Never twist His Word nor add or remove from it, but stay connected to Him day and night with a sincere heart and ask Him every desire of your heart in faith. Yes, as you do, you will be like a tree planted by the rivers of water and the Sun of righteousness will shine upon you. Every step shall turn to a blessing for you! People shall offer themselves freely to assist you. Thanksgiving shall fill your mouth. You will have an enlargement of heart from the God for all possibilities. Morning by morning, your light shall shine forth because you are a favoured of the Lord. Every day, the Sun shall shine and overshadow you. Rejoice evermore in His Light! Surely, no darkness shall have any hiding place in your life and family in Jesus' name.

THE POWER OF THE HOLY SPIRIT FOR EXPLOITS

At the time of our conversion, Christ reconciles us with the Father in love, forgiving all our sins and cleansing us from all unrighteousness. He removes the guilt of sin and makes us as new creatures. "Therefore if any man be in Christ, he is a new creature: old things are passed away; behold, all things are become new" (2 Corinthians 5:17). Not only are we made children of God, but we also have a measure of holiness and the Holy Spirit in us (John 14:17; Romans 8:14-16).

However, above these, God wants to impart His life into us so that we may be totally conformed to the image of Christ. He makes provision for our sanctification or purity of heart in Christ Jesus. After the believer is sanctified or set apart, God offers him the fullness of His power to do exploits. This is God's plan for His children and He promised, "But ye shall receive power, after that the Holy Ghost is come upon you: and ye shall be witnesses unto me both in Jerusalem, and in all Judaea, and in Samaria, and unto the uttermost part of the earth" (Acts 1:8).

For the believer who sincerely desires the power of the Holy Ghost and His gifts, the promises of God's willingness to give and His provision for the experience provides a solid basis for us to seek it earnestly. "And it shall come to pass afterward, that I will pour out my spirit upon all flesh; and your sons and your daughters shall prophesy, your old men shall dream dreams, your young men shall see visions: And also upon the servants and upon the handmaids in those days will I pour out my spirit (Joel 2:28-29).

From some Scriptural evidences, the initial evidence of the Holy Spirit baptism is the speaking of tongues. However, receiving the Holy Spirit is more than speaking in tongues. The power of God that accompanies that experience equips the believer to do exploits for the Lord. There are many who claim to have the Holy Spirit baptism, yet, the power is conspicuously missing in their lives and ministry. The Holy Spirit can accomplish the following in a believer's life:

- The Holy Spirit equips the believer to resist the devil and gives victory in the time of temptation (Matthew 4:1-4, 10-11; John 14:26; Romans 8:2).
- The Unction empowers the Christian to do fruitful services unto the Lord (Acts 1:8; Luke 24:49; 1 Corinthians 12:7-11).
- The Holy Ghost helps the saints in prayer (Romans 8:26-27; Zechariah 12:10).
- The Spirit illuminates, inspires and reveals the deep things of God to the believer (2 Peter 1:21; John 16:13-15; 1 Corinthians 2:9-12).
- The Spirit of truth guides the believer into all truth (John 14:26, 15:26; 16:13).
- The Spirit of God comforts and counsels the Christian (Isaiah 11:1-2; Acts 13:2).
- The Spirit of holiness equips the believer with the fruit of the Spirit (Galatians 5:22-23).

Only a man of the Spirit can do exploits for the Lord. Certainly, you can if you will determine to keep your spiritual battery charged constantly. The truth is that you cannot be effective and efficient in God's service without being full of the Holy Spirit. Ordinary vessels can only produce ordinary results. You cannot contribute maximally to God's Kingdom without being full of the Holy Ghost. Besides, you will constantly renew yourself by waiting upon the Lord in prayers.

The anointing or empowerment by the Spirit is what can lead to extraordinary performance in God's service and doing exploits for Him! Renewal, revival and restoration are not possible without being filled with the Spirit of God. Therefore, there is an urgent need for every believer to receive this provision and blessing because the harvest is now plenteous but the labourers are few; therefore, receive ye the Holy Ghost (John 20:22). Serve the Lord faithfully with all your heart and for the rest of your life.

Unfortunately, most people think everything will end here on earth. On that note, they go ahead and do whatever they like, leaving the essential things for the things that have no eternal value. Nothing moves them to show compassion for others despite the fact that God has blessed them; they use the gifts of God anyhow. Admittedly, does this attitude describe you? If yes, a change is needed because, you need to serve with the mind of Christ and eternity in view!

Chapter 9

REDEMPTIVE NAMES OF GOD ALMIGHTY

"The name of the LORD is a strong tower: the righteous runneth into it, and is safe" (Proverbs 18:10). The name of God has the power to work miracles (Mark 9:37-39). The name of the Lord is above all other names and powers (Philippians 2:9) and it is through the name of God that we can have victory in the battles of life (Psalms 20:5-8). God's names enumerated below have irresistible and redemptive powers to save people from sin, sickness and Satan when truly surrender to Jesus.

YAHWEH

"And I appeared unto Abraham, unto Isaac, and unto Jacob, by the name of God Almighty, but by my name JEHOVAH was I not known to them" (Exodus 6:3). This name was given to Moses when God was strengthening His hands and heart in the task of bringing the children of Israel out of Egyptian bondage. It was with this name that Moses wrought many wonders.

There is no doubt that God's name commands awesome power when used correctly, judiciously and righteously.

JEHOVAH JIREH: THE LORD MY PROVIDER

God is the Provider of good things. "And Isaac spake unto Abraham his father, and said, My father: and he said, Here am I, my son. And he said, Behold the fire and the wood: but where is the lamb for a burnt offering? And Abraham said, My son, God will provide himself a lamb for a burnt offering: so they went both of them together… And Abraham called the name of that place Jehovah-Jireh: as it is said to this day, In the mount of the LORD it shall be seen" (Genesis 22:7-8, 14).

When Abraham was confronted by his son Isaac (on their way to the sacrificial altar) as to the whereabouts of the ram for the burnt offering, he did reply his son by words and acts of faith when he told Isaac that God would provide; and God surely provided. Hence Abraham named the place where God miraculously provided himself a provider of good things "Jehovah Jireh." He is the great provider of good things at all times. Do not doubt the awesome power of God but rejoice in Him always and keep believing Him for His divine intervention in your affairs.

The name Jehovah Jireh means the Lord shall provide all our needs if we can trust and call upon Him. We shall, therefore, use the name Jehovah Jireh to pray that:

- The Lord may open the windows of heaven for needful resources – money and materials - to meet our personal, family and ministry needs.

- God may give knowledge, wisdom and retentive memory to our children to excel in their academic and secular endeavors.

- God, by His infinite mercy, will grant that the whole family may experience God's prosperity this year.

- God may grant us uncommon favour and bless the works of our hands abundantly this year and beyond.

- God may give us divine strength and grace to love and serve Him acceptably all the days of our lives (Luke 1:74-75). "But my God shall supply all your need according to his riches in glory by Christ Jesus" (Philippians 4:19).

JEHOVAH NISSI: THE LORD MY SHIELD OR BANNER

"And the LORD said unto Moses, write this for a memorial in a book, and rehearse it in the ears of Joshua: for I will utterly put out the remembrance of Amalek from under heaven. And Moses built an altar, and called the name of its Jehovah-Nissi" (Exodus 17:14-15). This name was not given to Moses until God had conquered Amalek in their fight against Israel. Although Joshua and the Israelites were engaged in the battle against the Amalekites, Moses had to sit afar off with his hands held up and high throughout the duration of the war up until the time when the Amalekites were defeated. Indeed, Jehovah proved Himself to be strong because the Israelites won the battle against Amalekites; hence Moses named the place Jehovah Nissi. God is not partial and He is still the same. If God is the stronghold of the Israelites, why can't He be yours and mine too today? According to the Book of Exodus, the Lord is my shield or defense. The Lord is my banner. Jehovah Nissi protects and defends God's people. Therefore, let's pray, and proclaim this loudly: "Surely, the Lord shall deliver me from the snare of the fowler and from the noisome pestilence."

Pray that:

- The Lord becomes your refuge and fortress in the storms of life (Psalms 91:2).
- The Lord protects you from every evil work and assault of the wicked (Psalms 91:3).
- The Lord hides your family in His secret pavilion and keeps you from every danger. There shall no evil befall you neither shall any sickness nor plague come near your dwellings (Psalms 91:10).

Moreover, God will set confusion in your enemies' camp! Under no circumstances shall any of them escape! None of them shall stand, but they all shall be scattered. Divine judgement shall be unleashed on them. As you mention 'Jesus,' they shall be confused and you shall have total victory in Jesus' Name.

JEHOVAH SHALOM: THE LORD IS PEACE

"And the LORD said unto him, Peace be unto thee; fear not: thou shalt not die. Then Gideon built an altar there unto the LORD, and called it Jehovah-shalom: unto this day it is yet in Ophrah of the Abiezrites" (Judges 6:23-24). This name was given to Gideon when Jehovah God made peace with Israel after they had sinned and were delivered into the hands of the Midianites (Judges 6:1-7). When you are afflicted and surrounded by enemies due to your faith in Christ or you are experiencing problems of any kind and you pray, calling on the name of Jehovah Shalom, peace would be restored unto you. The Lord Jehovah Shalom can restore peace in the church, government and the whole world at large. The name Jehovah Shalom means the Lord our peace.

Let's pray that:

- The God of peace may grant that His peace would reign supreme in our life, family and nation throughout this year and beyond.
- The peace of God should rule the families of God's people and that the Lord would reign without rival in our spouses and children.
- The hope of the devil and his cohorts regarding our homes, works and our spiritual life be disappointed and dashed.
- The peace of God is released unto every Christian going through torments, afflictions and persecution. May "The LORD bless thee, and keep thee: The LORD make his face shine upon thee, and be gracious unto thee: The LORD lift up his countenance upon thee, and give thee peace" (Numbers 6:24-26).

JEHOVAH SHAMMAH: THE LORD IS THERE

"It was round about eighteen thousand measures: and the name of the city from that day shall be, The LORD is there" (Ezekiel 48:35). The Holy name was given to Ezekiel after the Lord had commanded him to divide the land among the tribes of Israel. Ezekiel, having therefore done according to

God's commandment named the city Jehovah Shammah, meaning Jehovah is there. We shall therefore pray that, because the Lord Jehovah is there for me:

· No weapon formed against me shall prosper.
· The presence of the Lord in my life shall destroy all the moves of the wicked against my life.
· Every place the sole of my feet shall tread shall be given unto me.
· I will possess the gates of my enemies.

JEHOVAH TSIDKENU: OUR RIGHTEOUS GOD

"Behold, the days come, saith the LORD, that I will raise unto David a righteous Branch, and a King shall reign and prosper, and shall execute judgment and justice in the earth. In his days Judah shall be saved, and Israel shall dwell safely: and this is his name whereby he shall be called, THE LORD OUR RIGHTEOUSNESS" (Jeremiah 23:5-6). God has absolute power to put His righteousness in you and your family members if you pray. The Lord is known by His name: Jehovah Tsidkenu meaning: The Lord our righteousness. The name is capable of inputting God's holy nature into His children.

We shall therefore pray that:
· The Lord establishes His righteousness in you– Isaiah 54:14.
· Your life shall be free from oppression and terror of men and Satan.
· Your life shall become a praise forever.

- Lord, let your people be rooted and grounded in righteousness.
- O Lord, help us to put on the breastplate of righteousness as our main weapon for fighting the enemy. "But upon mount Zion shall be deliverance, and there shall be holiness; and the house of Jacob shall possess their possessions" (Obadiah 1:17).

You will surely possess your all possessions as you confess your sins, forsake them and trust God. You shall receive the miracle of God's mercy over your life and family; and holiness will be your lifestyles in Jesus' mighty name!

JEHOVAH RAPHA: THE LORD THAT HEALS

"And said, If thou wilt diligently hearken to the voice of the LORD thy God, and wilt do that which is right in his sight, and wilt give ear to his commandments, and keep all his statutes, I will put none of these diseases upon thee, which I have brought upon the Egyptians: for I am the LORD that healeth thee" (Exodus 15:25-26). After Moses and Israelites had crossed the Red Sea, they went in the wilderness for three days without water. On the third day, they came to Marah and found water which was bitter and undrinkable. Jehovah Rapha proved Himself as a true Healer when he commanded Moses to heal the water and make it drinkable. Moses healed the water by casting a particular tree that the Lord showed him into the water. The water became sweet or portable and good for drinking and the Israelites drank. Jehovah Rapha can heal all sicknesses and input divine health.

Therefore pray thus:

· That because the Lord is your healer, every seed of illness or any infirmity in your system, be uprooted and burnt with the fire of God now.

· That the Lord will restore health to anyone sick in your family and among the brethren; and heal every wound (Jeremiah 30:17).

· That the Lord will cure any illness or incurable sickness in any of the brethren lying on the sick bed.

· That the Lord Jehovah Rapha will give healing as bread to all our sick brethren.

Thank God for His covenant provisions through His Word! Undeniably, if you can appropriate these promises by faith, you will be healed. The evil spirits that cause infirmities will go out of you, sicknesses will vanish and diseases will depart from you. At the mention of the Name of Jesus, all knees would bow. Yes, healing and health are yours in Jesus' mighty name! Surely, God is able to heal all sicknesses and diseases. Unwavering faith in Him can procure your health as there is no impossibility with God. He can heal you! Divine healing is assured and all you need do is call upon Him. You will be made whole in Jesus' Name. Hear the Word of God, 'You will not experience any Egyptian diseases.' Understand, that there is an Almighty God Whose name is Jehovah Rapha!

Thinking about your health challenges? There is hope for the hopeless and for you too because God cares about your health. Everything about your health is provided for in

God's Word. Sickness is from the pit of hell, but God wants you healed, hale, hearty and healthy! Divine healing is yours to claim by faith for all His promises are yea and Amen (2 Corinthians 1:20). Yes, you will be made whole by His stripes in Jesus' Name!

EL-SHADDAI: GOD ALMIGHTY

"And when Abram was ninety years old and nine, the LORD appeared to Abram, and said unto him, I am the Almighty God; walk before me, and be thou perfect" (Genesis 17:1). El-Shaddai means God Almighty. The manifestation of this Holy name was first made to Abram when he was ninety-nine years old and had lost hope of having a child through Sarah his wife. It was after the Lord had made himself known to Abram as God Almighty that he promised him a son and there is nothing impossible for Him to do.

Events later proved El-Shaddai right in the sense that Sarah, at old age of ninety years, conceived and gave birth to Isaac. If El-Shaddai the Almighty can do this wonder for an old woman, what else can He not do for you? God is still asking you the same question today, He is waiting for your answer. "Behold, I am the LORD, the God of all flesh: is there anything too hard for me?" (Jeremiah 32:27).

Absolutely nothing is too hard for God to do. This name is also for those who have lost hope in life. There is nothing impossible for God. Surely, God is a great Helper in times of trouble. All you need to do is to trust and believe Him. Trusting God is a motivation to calling upon Him. Under no circumstances will He ignore a trusting seeker. Remember God first, no matter how daunting your situation! Do not despise a sincere prayer of faith asking for His help. As you do, He will surely act! Yes, God can help you in your troubles. Call upon Him.

ADONAI: THE LORD OR THE MASTER

This name was used in the Bible more than 300 times, most especially by Abraham, the father of faith. Abraham, in his usual mode of highly exalting Jehovah God, counted it not enough respect to address God as Jehovah on his way to show how great and mighty Jehovah God was to him (Abraham), so, he usually referred to God as Adonai Jehovah, my Lord Jehovah. In other words, Jehovah was not only his God but also his Lord. He is the Master and Ruler of all affairs in the kingdom of men (Daniel 4:17). "Ye call me Master and Lord: and ye say well; for so I am. If I then, your Lord and Master, have washed your feet; ye also ought to wash one another's feet." (John 13:13-14; Read Matthew 23:8).

Surely, you need God every day. Wake up early to commune with Him. Nothing should stand as a barrier or hindrance. Devotional hours are spiritual moments that you must not miss daily. Being alone with God daily helps your close intimacy with Him. Yes, quiet time with God is an exercise you must not miss on daily basis." The LORD will perfect that which concerneth me: thy mercy, O LORD, endureth forever: forsake not the works of thine own hands" (Psalms 138:8). All His promises are yea and amen. There is no shadow of turning with God and His Words of power are unmistakable. Rest on His promises which cannot fail. Do as He has said and never doubt Him. All His promises shall surely come to pass! - Yes, nothing shall fail in His Word of promise. He will perform them in your life.

THE GREAT NAME OF JESUS CHRIST

"And she shall bring forth a son, and thou shalt call his name JESUS: for he shall save his people from their sins...Wherefore God also hath highly exalted him, and given him a name which is above every name: That at the name of Jesus every knee should bow, of things in heaven, and things in earth, and things under the earth; And that every tongue should confess that Jesus Christ is Lord, to the glory of God the Father" (Matthew 1:21; Philippians 2:9-11).

Jesus redeemed us from all sins as He is our Redeemer and Saviour. All the redemptive names of the Almighty God are wrapped up in one name, the Mighty NAME of JESUS! In other words, the name of Jesus operates with mighty power in each redemptive name of God and He demonstrated the attributes of God in His earthly ministry. This name of Jesus creates expectancy and it is the power of the Christian and the church as a whole. Jesus Christ is our Saviour, Lord and God (Acts 4:12; Colossians 2:8-11; Hebrews 1:8).

The miracle you will receive depends on your faithfulness to His Word and faith in the Name of Jesus today if you believe. At the mention of His name, sicknesses, infirmities, storms of life, diseases and every lack have to bend their knees and leave to confess and confirm that Jesus Christ is the Lord to the glory of God the Father!

Above all, Jesus is our righteousness, the hope of eternal life for all Christians. "These words spake Jesus, and lifted up his eyes to heaven, and said, Father, the hour is come; glorify thy Son, that thy Son also may glorify thee: As thou hast given him power over all flesh, that he should give eternal life to as many as thou hast given him. And this is life eternal, that they might know thee the only true God, and Jesus Christ, whom thou hast sent" (John 17:1-3). You should begin to build up our confidence and trust in this great name and prepare for miracles needed in every moment of your life.

We are nothing without Jesus, for God the Father has highly exalted Him by given Him a name that is above every other name that can ever exist in life. His name is JESUS! Join me to shout it loud and clear three times - JESUS! JESUS!! JESUS!!! He is the only Lord and Saviour of the whole world. Praise ye the LORD!!! Not only that, He assured us that He will do whatever we shall ask in His name. "And whatsoever ye shall ask in my name, that will I do, that the Father may be glorified in the Son. If ye shall ask any thing in my name, I will do it" (John 14:13-14). This Scripture confirmed that He has given us authority to cast out demons in His name too (Mark 16:17-18). All strongholds of opposing forces can be cast down and out in the name of Jesus!

Many people claim to be in Christ, yet they still walk in darkness! On daily basis such folks are in warfare with Satan and the powers of darkness! No doubt, the truth is that Christ's life is not in them! The divine instruction for such people is to recheck their lives and relationship with Christ! A life of Christ brings total freedom! Yes, when old things are passed away, all things become new!

You must not betray or deny Jesus Christ in any situation or challenges of life." Jesus saith to him, He that is washed needeth not save to wash his feet, but is clean every whit: and ye are clean, but not all... I speak not of you all: I know whom I have chosen: but that the Scripture may be fulfilled, He that eateth bread with me hath lifted up his heel against me" (John 13:10, 18).

Some friends of Christ are betraying and denying Him daily! Regrettably, many Christians are drifting from the gospel truths. Increasingly, false teachings and preaching are the order of the day. Deceivers are increasing in the Christian fold. Yes, you must stand out in the defense of the faith! The Word of God says, "Thy word is a lamp unto my feet, and a light unto my path...For the commandment is a lamp; and the law is light; and reproofs of instruction are the way of life" (Psalms 119:105; Proverbs 6:23).

Be a true follower of our Lord Jesus Christ and be a light in the dark world. Sinners are in the dark. Anyone in the light must walk like Christ. The light always shines in the darkness! Unfortunately, a lot of Christians still walk in darkness. Remaining in Christ is a means of overcoming darkness. Daily search of the Scriptures is also a step to lighten one's path. Are you in a light? Be a shining light by abiding in Christ and in His Word!

Chapter 10

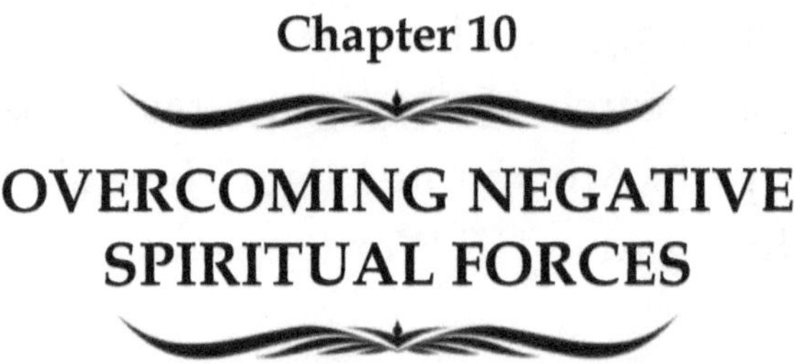

OVERCOMING NEGATIVE SPIRITUAL FORCES

"For though we walk in the flesh, we do not war after the flesh: (For the weapons of our warfare are not carnal, but mighty through God to the pulling down of strong holds;) Casting down imaginations, and every high thing that exalteth itself against the knowledge of God, and bringing into captivity every thought to the obedience of Christ" (2 Corinthians 10:3-5).

The whole world is full of darkness (evil). The Bible even describes it as "...this present evil world" (Galatians 1:4) that lieth in wickedness (1 John 5:19) whose god is Satan which the Bible calls the "power of darkness" (Colossians 1:13) - the enemy of God and the archenemy of man.

From the outset, there is need to debunk some erroneous beliefs about the identity of Satan. He is not a mere evil power, influence or the negation of good but an intelligent spiritual personality, ruler of a vast kingdom and god of this world who rules through principalities, powers, rulers of darkness of this world (thrones) and spiritual wickedness in high places (a host of demons and evil spirits in the second heaven). Fellow citizens of Christ's Kingdom, the point has to be emphasized that spiritual battle is real but you will surely prevail through Christ.

ACTIVITIES OF NEGATIVE SPIRITUAL FORCES

For every original, there is a counterfeit. In order for Satan to achieve his diabolical intentions, he has a tight network of organized demonic spirits with specialized skills in areas of evil activities (Ephesians 6:12). These constitute his hosts which are responsible for building strongholds in the lives of men. Strongholds are the bulwarks or fortresses built by the devil against his prey to keep them in perpetual slavery or bondage. The emissaries of darkness engage in ceaseless warfare with believers in a bid to hinder, tempt, deceive, discourage, defeat, oppress and destroy them. Is this not what the Bible says in John 10:10? "The thief (devil) cometh not, but for to steal, and to kill, and to destroy:…"

Demons, evil spirits and human agents (witches, wizards, necromancers, diviners, herbalists, magicians, witch doctors and false prophets) are Satan's tools who wreak untold havoc on people's lives, hinder progress, cause strange happenings, mysterious deaths and other misfortunes all too suddenly in individual lives. This could be in form of chronic sickness or oppression caused by the devil that defies medication as in the case of the woman bound for 18 years by Satan (Luke 13:16). It could be a calculated attempt by the devil to hinder one from rising up, like the plan of the Jews to hinder or discredit the resurrection of Christ (Matthew 27:62-66) and the territorial demonic spirits machinations in the case of the prince of the kingdom of Persia which hindered the answers to Daniel's prayer for 21 days (Daniel 10:12-13).

The opposition of Bar-jesus during Paul's ministration to Sergius Paulus was a stronghold that could have hindered his salvation if Paul had not taken authority over him (Acts 13:6-10). It could be likened to a wall of barrier hindering the penetration of the gospel in certain communities just as the Jericho wall that was straightly shut up because of the children of Israel so that no one went out and no one came in (Joshua 6:1; Numbers 13:19). It could be likened to an Esau (in spiritual sense) behind a Jacob to keep him in the bondage of fear of death and in a spot without further progress in life (Genesis 32:6-8). It could be a persistent activity of demonic spirits designed to weaken one's hand and slow the progress of one's projects or endeavours in life just as Sanballat and Tobiah stood against Nehemiah (Nehemiah 4:1-3).

Therefore, Satan, not God, is the source and cause of all evil misfortunes (John 8:44). But "...thanks be unto God, which always causeth us to triumph in Christ, and maketh manifest the savour of his knowledge by us in every place" (2 Corinthians 2:14). "Blotting out the handwriting of ordinances that was against us, which was contrary to us, and took it out of the way, nailing it to his cross. And having spoiled principalities and powers, he made a shew of them openly, triumphing over them in it" (Colossians 2:14-15). Jesus overcame Satan on the cross when he shouted the greatest Victor's cry ever, "It is finished" (John 19:30). This means, mission accomplished! Satan is defeated! Hallelujah! As a result, the believer has the authority to rebuke and destroy Satan's works. His faith becomes energized and fortified in the battle against strongholds through prevailing prayers in the mighty name of Jesus. There are diverse reasons why individuals are oppressed. Some of these are:

Sin, an open door and major cause of oppression. "He that committeth sin is of the devil; for the devil sinneth from the beginning. For this purpose, the Son of God was manifested, that he might destroy the works of the devil" (1 John 3:8). Sin such as bitterness, wrath, envy, jealousy, pride, lying, resentment, uncontrolled anger and desire for revenge opens doors for demonic oppression.

Without exception, those who have become involved in any form of occultism usually suffer satanic oppression. Besides, it is against God's will for his people. This is the reason we speak so vehemently against occultism and witchcraft (Deuteronomy 18:9-12).

Traumatic experiences, weakness, emotional crisis, feeling of not being loved, loneliness, fear or even illnesses can bring oppression. There is also a belief that hard luck and mysterious occurrences may be inherited.

Religious errors such as spiritism, false doctrines and Christian cults (Sectarianism, denominationalism, Rosicrucian, Theosophy et al) constitute open doors for demons.

The way out is genuine repentance and renunciation of all cults or of any involvement with satanic practices. Also, we must learn to forgive and forget all past offences and offenders! We must right all forms of wrongs and be a peacemaker! There is need to intercede for those who may have offended you and you do not have to delay reconciliation with those who have wrong you! Ask God for grace to forgive them and to pardon your offences too! Yes, free your mind from the pains you have been causing yourself.

Demonic spirits operate in various ways. They harass (Ephesians 6:12); enslave (Romans 8:15); entice (James 1:14-15); deceive (1 Timothy 4:1-2); torment (2 Timothy 1:7; 1 John 4:18); drive or compel (Luke 8:29) and defile (Titus 1:15). Their great distinctive mark is restlessness. They can affect someone's thoughts, emotions and attitudes leading to indecision and procrastination.

Here are some Scriptural examples of the afflicted: The Gadarene demoniac (Mark 5:1-20); Mary Magdalene (Luke 8:2); The Syrophoenician woman's daughter (Matthew 15:22-28); The woman with the issue of blood (Mark 13:11-16); The man with 38 years of impotence (John 5:5-14); the Shunammites' son's death (2 King 4:18-20), Elimelech's and his sons' death (Ruth 1:1-5); the man who had been vexed with deaf and dumb spirits from childhood (Mark 9:17-27); the man born blind (John 9:1-7); the damsel with the spirit of divination (Acts 16:16-18); Job (Job 1 and 2) and numerous others who were grievously tormented by devils and unclean spirits (Mark 1:23). The good news about them is that they all were delivered and raised back to life except the case of Elimelech's family which was a consequence of self-management. Today as well, many obsessed or oppressed or even possessed people are being liberated through the divine intervention of Jesus Christ.

NEVER DESPAIR IN ANY SITUATION

"How long wilt thou forget me, O LORD? forever? how long wilt thou hide thy face from me? How long shall I take counsel in my soul, having sorrow in my heart daily? how long shall mine enemy be exalted over me? Consider and hear me, O LORD my God: lighten mine eyes, lest I sleep the sleep of death; Lest mine enemy say, I have prevailed against him; and those that trouble me rejoice when I am moved. But I have trusted in thy mercy; my heart shall rejoice in thy salvation. I will sing unto the LORD, because he hath dealt bountifully with me" (Psalms 13:1-6).

The Scriptures revealed here that David was depressed with the thought that God has forsaken him but he was wrong! This is the situation of most people when faced with challenges of life, especially when it appears God is silent to their prayers as they prayed. For this reason, some would like to get what they wanted by all means outside God's plan. Hence the step would cause them to fall into the hands of false prophets or messengers of the devil for solution. But Satan's solution will lead to suffering and everlasting perdition with him in the lake of fire.

God knows His own thoughts concerning His children and makes things beautiful for them in His own time. Therefore,

God's silence or withdrawal has its way of jerking the hearts of sincere seekers to thirst, hunger and come closer to Him. God is not partial, even those with a long-standing relationship with God in prayers are not immune to this experience; so was the Psalmist and of course, everyone. Delay to the answer of the prayer of the Psalmist made him to think that he had been abandoned and left alone in misery. Sorrow of heart and loneliness became his companions.

Notwithstanding, the Psalmist made several attempts to escape from his problems and difficulties but to no avail. The more he tried, the more he failed. Interestingly, these frustrating circumstances did not stop him from recalling himself to God's remembrance. He felt his enemies will soon rejoice over him if left without immediate solution. But he encouraged himself in the Lord and bounced back from a state of despair, despondency and spiritual deadness to life, hope and confidence after all. Here, we have many lessons to learn from the Psalmist as Christians. In every challenge we may face in life, God will not leave His people in despair. He may sometimes seem withdrawn and unheard, yet He hears, understand and will rise to their aid. Importunate praying coupled with faith in God's goodness and mercy will once again give voice to another Psalms of David.

FAITH THAT OVERCOMES FEAR

"There were they in great fear, where no fear was: for God hath scattered the bones of him that encampeth against thee: thou hast put them to shame, because God hath despised them...For whatsoever is born of God overcometh the world: and this is the victory that overcometh the world, even our faith: (Psalms 53:5; 1 John 5:4). Many people are afraid of what may never happen because their hearts are failing them of the fear of unknown and when fear comes, it paralyses our faith with unnecessary panic, fright and torment. This destroys our confidence and demobilizes us. Instead, we must resist fear in our hearts and strive to possess faith that overcomes fear (1 John 4:18).

Fear is a spirit, and it works in the heart and soul to weaken the inner man and get to the brain. After salvation, God has given us the spirit of power, love and sound mind (2 Timothy 1:7). Fear is from Satan; he brings fear to make us stop believing in order to detach and isolate us from God so as to deal ruthlessly with us. Satan knows that through faith in God, we can move the Lord into our situation to do the miraculous.

Faith is a strong persuasion that leads to having the desires of our hearts from God. It is the eyes of the mind, the reality of those things that are discerned by physical senses. Hence Christian life is a life of faith. "But without faith it is impossible to please him: for he that cometh to God must believe that he is, and that he is a rewarder of them that diligently seek him" (Hebrews 11:6). It takes faith to begin the Christian journey, to continue and to finish well. Faith is pivotal and significant to the Christian life. Through faith, we have peace with God and possess the power of God.

No Christian can pray and receive answers to prayers nor please God without faith. Walking and living by faith is a daily routine of Christian pilgrims on earth. Whether we are passing through life challenges or in plenty, we must walk by faith and not by sight in order to please God.

The fact remains that you cannot win life's battle without spiritual weapons because your enemies are not human but spiritual beings. Engaging them in battle requires using relevant weapons. Spiritual warfare needs potent spiritual weapons. Defeated Christians are those who fail to use them. Armours are for both defensive and offensive use. You must sharpen and use them for your daily victory. Wars against your life shall come to an end and the enemies running after you shall be silenced. Do not fear their threatening or bow to their entreaties but engage them in the Name of the Lord. Submit to God, resist the adversary and divine help shall come to you. Always put your trust and confidence in God and you will triumph over all oppositions in Jesus' Name.

Never give up; there is hope for you! Opportunity can always come your way when you least expected. Very many people have missed their opportunities in life because they gave up too soon. Endurance plus faith in God are your sustaining keys. More importantly, always note that delay is never a denial. Do not get easily distracted; it is tough people that do last. Always renew your trust and confidence in the Lord regardless of the situation, never give up and the Lord will give you an answer of peace. Everything will be all right as Christ has paid all the price for your sake. Just look up to Him for He cares for you. Make no provision for doubts since God is able. Build your hope and confidence in Him, encourage yourself in the Lord always and God shall turn it around for better.

Faith in God and in His Word are spiritual tools that can get us out of spiritual blackouts. Resting on the flesh produces no tangible results. Insightfulness and vision are useful keys against blackouts. Divine inspiration is an unction to function tool that you need also! A grain of sin brings darkness and pains. "It is the spirit that quickeneth; the flesh profiteth nothing: the words that I speak unto you, they are spirit, and they are life" (John 6:63). Yes, pray that God should get you out of spiritual blackouts.

Again, there is need to wait for God's time! Use of time can best be planned by God, so, let Him be part of your plans. Everyone is a product of time: time for birth, to live, for activities and to die. So, wait for God's time; don't be in haste. Daily pray to God for guidance! After knowing God's will, you still need patience. Yes, wait patiently for God. Don't fret, fear or get worried.

The desire of your heart shall be granted in this season. For every expectation in your heart shall the Lord grant you answer. Christ became poor so that you can become rich. He died for your sake and everything you desire is possible through Jesus Christ. Make your requests known unto Him in prayers and He shall answer you. But you must come to Him with faith and full assurance that He will answer you. An end must come to your lack and poverty soon enough.

You must rise above all forms of reproaches. Reach forth to the Lord in a prayer of faith! He will surprise you and make your joy full in this season.

Learn from David, who used a staff, a stone, a sling and trust in the Almighty God to defeat Goliath who had a sword, a spear and a shield. Even so, the Lord will arise on your behalf to destroy all that represent Goliath in your life in Jesus' name! Can God do it? Yes, He can. Come before Him with humility and faith! Kill your fears! The Eternal God knows all the battles confronting your life. Just boldly come to Him in prayers! He will grant you the victory. Mind you, God does not need swords, spears and shields to fight your battle because He is a Man of war. But you might say why the staff, stone and sling that David used then? The Lord can use insignificant things to confound the mighty.

Skills can be inspired and developed through God's special visitation. Undoubtedly, Bezaleel was such a vessel identified and empowered. It is noteworthy that he was also filled with the Spirit of God. (Please, read Exodus 35:30-35; 36:1-3). The Divine hand can locate you and touch you like Bezaleel if you can focus on God without distraction and prepare for His divine visitation. Ask the Lord to inspire you and empower you too. Yes, He is not partial but abundantly able to provide for you if you would make yourself available for His use.

Enough of the enemies terrorizing your life! This day they shall fall at the mention of the name of Jesus. Remember, our God is mighty in battle and He has never lost any battle. I pray that this day He will arise on your behalf and pull down every stronghold confronting your life in the mighty name of Jesus!!!

THE LIMITATIONS OF SATAN

Down through the ages, Satan has been overrated and his power blown out of proportion by religious infidels and the generality of mankind. Satan is a personal adversary to us all and no one is immune from his attacks and that of his imps, though. However terrible and devastatingly destructive Satan's operations, he is far more limited by his weaknesses which he always frantically hides from his unsuspecting victims and preys. It is only the spiritually inclined in Christ that are not ignorant of the devil's devices and they are the only ones who can effectively deal with him. In this regard, we shall highlight the many inhibitions and limitations of Lucifer, that old serpent, the dragon, the destroyer, the arch-enemy of God and man, the devil also known as Satan.

- Satan is NOT OMNISCIENT. He does not know everything or what you are thinking; he cannot read your mind but he knows whether you are righteous or sinful. Only God is omniscient and believers know more than Satan does - Job 1:7-12.

- Satan is NOT OMNIPRESENT. He cannot be at two places at a time but he has demons or representatives all over the world who works by proxy for him which make him seem ubiquitous. Sure, devils can transmogrify, transform or assume some other identities to deceive. 2 Corinthians 11:13-15 clearly expresses that *"For such are false apostles, deceitful workers, transforming themselves into the apostles of Christ. And no marvel; for Satan himself is transformed into an angel of light. Therefore it is no great thing if his ministers also be transformed as the ministers of righteousness; whose end shall be according to their works."*

- Satan is NOT OMNIPOTENT. After Satan was thrown out of Heaven, God did not revoke the devil's power or forces from him but gave believers all authority over Satan and his kingdom – Luke 10:1, 17-20 *"…Behold, I give unto you power to tread on serpents and scorpions, and over all the power of the enemy: and nothing shall by any means hurt you…"*

- Satan is NOT GREATER THAN MAN. No devil, angel or any other creature was made in God's image but man – Genesis 1:27. The Bible confirms that saints shall judge angels in 1 Corinthians 6:3, *"Know ye not that we shall judge angels? how much more things that pertain to this life?"* So, believers have the right to resist, rebuke and cast out the devil(s) – 1 Peter 5:9; James 4:7; Luke 9:1; Matthew 10:1, 8.

- Satan CANNOT REPENT, get saved or be forgiven. He is doomed forever to perdition and eternal destruction - Matthew 25:41. We are not told to feel sorry for Satan.

- Satan CANNOT STOP GOD from doing His work – Matthew 16:18; 2 Thessalonians 2:7.

- Satan CANNOT FORCE YOU TO SIN or use you as a robot without your permission or yielding your will-power to him. So, you cannot blame Satan - the tempter for the wicked things you do. God will hold you personally responsible for your sins – James 1:12-15; Ezekiel 18:4, 20 *"The soul that sinneth, it shall die. The son shall not bear the iniquity of the father, neither shall the father bear the iniquity of the son: the righteousness of the righteous shall be upon him, and the wickedness of the wicked shall be upon him."*

- Satan CANNOT POSSESS A BORN AGAIN BIBLE BELIEVER. Romans 8:9 *"But ye are not in the flesh, but in the Spirit, if so be that the Spirit of God dwell in you. Now if any man have not the Spirit of Christ, he is none of his.*

- Satan CANNOT TAKE YOUR SALVATION AWAY but you can fall from grace into perdition if you are not watchful - John 10:27-29 *"...And I give unto them eternal life; and they shall never perish, neither shall any man pluck them out of my hand. My Father, which gave them me, is greater than all; and no man is able to pluck them out of my Father's hand..."* Galatians 5:4 *"Christ is become of no effect unto you, whosoever of you are justified by the law; ye are fallen from grace."*

- Satan CANNOT CAST ANYONE INTO HELL OR THE LAKE OF FIRE; only God does. The devil and his angels will suffer punishment in Hell as well as unrepentant human beings – Matthew 25:41, 46 *"Then shall he say also unto them on the left hand, Depart from me, ye cursed, into everlasting fire, prepared for the devil and his angels: And these shall go away into everlasting punishment: but the righteous into life eternal."* Luke 12:4-5; Revelation 20:10 *"And the devil that deceived them was cast into the lake of fire and brimstone, where the beast and the false prophet are, and shall be tormented day and night for ever and ever."*

- Satan CANNOT WIN. Ultimately, he is a loser – Romans 20:16 *"And the God of peace shall bruise Satan under your feet shortly. The grace of our Lord Jesus Christ be with you. Amen."* Revelation 12:7-10.

Holy believers in Christ are vested with Divine authority to resist the devil, rebuke him, bind him, bruise his head and cast him out decisively. Satan knows this and he shudders, bows and flees from a Christian who knows his rights. At this juncture, it is trite to say that saints need to marshal and deploy spiritual weapons appropriately in order to achieve constant victory over Satan and his cohorts.

SUPERNATURAL WEAPONS FOR VICTORY

"For though we walk in the flesh, we do not war after the flesh: (For the weapons of our warfare are not carnal, but mighty through God to the pulling down of strong holds;) Casting down imaginations, and every high thing that exalteth itself against the knowledge of God, and bringing into captivity every thought to the obedience of Christ; And having in a readiness to revenge all disobedience, when your obedience is fulfilled" (2 Corinthians 10:3-6).

It is a settled fact that believers in this world are in a continuous battle ground. Forces exist both within and without which the believer needs to contend with and overcome on a daily basis if our desire and aspiration to spend eternity with God will not end up as a mirage or a mere wish like that of Balaam, who wished to die the death of the righteous but ended up his life as a backslidden prophet because he was unable to conquer his fleshly lust for riches (Numbers 23:10; 31:8). But the Lord our God has given us the assurance of victory, having provided for us sure weapons of warfare that are adequate and appropriate for everlasting victory. However, to fight manfully onward and be an eventual victor, there is need to have a good understanding of the battle, the available weapons, the source, as well as the means of acquiring and deploying the weapons for constant victory.

Ignorance about facts and features of spiritual warfare has destroyed many a Christian today and made them continuous victims and preys in the hands of the devil and his cohorts. While some pretend or assume that there is no battle to fight, there are those who mistake the battle for a physical one and are therefore, employing physical means like appealing, clinching, compensating, confronting and combating a physical agent of the enemy at one time or another, to no avail.

Ephesians 6:12, "For we wrestle not against flesh and blood, but against principalities, against powers, against the rulers of the darkness of this world, against spiritual wickedness in high places" revealed the battle to fight here: Combating the forces of Satan, sin and self (1 Peter 5:8; Hebrews 12:4; James 4:1). Contention to secure (what is at stake) - the eternal life of God in you (Luke 22:31). Constitution of the fight spiritually not physically (2 Corinthians 10:3; Ephesians 6:12).

Certainty of victory as Christ has assured us of victory (John 16:33). Condition for victory by putting on the whole armour of God (Ephesians 6:11-13) and Conscious commitment to be victorious (1 Peter 5:8).

The application of wrong weapons has always and will always result in utter failure in the battle of life. As the Scriptures revealed, carnal weapons cannot suffice for spiritual warfare, it only takes away our attention from God Who is our real help. "Thus, saith the LORD; Cursed be the man that trusteth in man, and maketh flesh his arm, and whose heart departeth from the LORD" (Jeremiah 17:5).

There are supernatural weapons, tested and trusted, that can never fail. These are referred to as "The whole armour of God." (For full details of the armour, I would encourage you to read my two books: 'Satanic Attacks and the Way out;' and 'Prevailing Prayers of Intercession and Supplication Guides'). The whole armour of God belongs to God and is given to whosoever wills and that is the reason for the unfailing nature of the weapons. They are:

- **Belt of Truth** (Ephesians 4:25; John 8:32).

- **Breastplate of Righteousness** (Isaiah 59:17; 1 John 3:7).

- **Boots of the Gospel of Peace** (Isaiah 52:7; Ephesians 6:15).

- **Shield of Faith** (1 John 5:4).

- **Helmet of Salvation** (Mark 16:15; 1 Thessalonians 5:8b).

- **Sword of the Spirit**, the Word of God (Hebrews 4:12).

- **Prayer** (Luke 18:1).

Belt of Truth: (Ephesians 4:25; John 8:32). The truth that Satan and his demons have been defeated on the cross of Calvary by our Lord Jesus Christ for all believers in Him is our greatest weapon. God has translated us into the Kingdom of His Son far above principalities and powers (Colossians 1:13-14). Therefore, Satan is under our feet and our war against him and his kingdom is from above; but he is only trying to manipulate us so as to bring us into the bondage of religion that is not real.

This truth about our full redemption is a potent weapon against Satan. It puts us in a position of mastery over the devil and his angels of darkness. All we need to do is to take authority over him and his cohorts, bind him, banish him to where he belongs and trample his forces under our feet each time he tries to rear up his ugly head. Believers have nothing to fear in the midst of any battle because this authority in the name of Jesus is assured by the Almighty God Who gave it to us to subdue this arch-enemy of humanity.

Breastplate of Righteousness: "*...having on the breastplate of righteousness*" (Ephesians 6:14). Obedience to God's Word and living by faith to please Him at all times shield our hearts and minds from satanic arrows of guilt, doubt, fear and condemnation. A soldier without the breastplate violates the rule of protection and may receive a deadly attack in the area of the chest instantaneously. Sin is a transgression against God's Word and it makes us vulnerable to such attacks of the devil. On the contrary, righteousness will fortify us against the wiles of the devil.

"We know that whosoever is born of God sinneth not; but he that is begotten of God keepeth himself, and that wicked one toucheth him not" (1 John 5:18).

Boots of the Gospel of Peace: *"The Lord gave the word: great was the company of those that published it… And your feet shod with the preparation of the gospel of peace"* (Psalm 68:11; Ephesians 6:15). The gospel of peace is the gospel of liberty, freedom and deliverance that brought peace with God and men. Just like the shoes of ancient soldiers were specially made to grip the ground in the battle, we stand firm in the Lord and engage in war with the devil (not men) to liberate the soul of men, as our shoes remain in the gospel of peace.

Shield of Faith: We are together in the battle against a common foe but the shield of faith is a sure defence against the principalities and powers. It is the spiritual shield of the Lord that helps us prevail over the devil. It is an indispensable part of the Christian armour that protects us from attacks against the truth and by which we quench the fiery darts of the wicked. *"Above all, taking the shield of faith, wherewith ye shall be able to quench all the fiery darts of the wicked"* Ephesians 6:16).

Helmet of Salvation: *"And take the helmet of salvation…"* (Ephesians 6:17). The head is the primary target of the enemy in every battle and the helmet protects the head from piercing objects and the sword. The mind of believers is the primary target of the devil to weaken their faith and bring them down in defeat. *"Which hope we have as an anchor of the* soul, both sure and steadfast, and which entereth into that within the veil" (Hebrew 6:19).

Sword of the Spirit: *"…the sword of the Spirit, which is the word of God… For the word of God is quick, and powerful, and sharper than any two-edged sword, piercing even to the dividing asunder of soul and spirit, and of the joints and marrow, and is a discerner of the thoughts and intents of the heart"* (Ephesians 6:17; Hebrew 4:12). The sword of the spirit is two-edged and it is meant to be used defensively and offensively by faith. It pierces and does damage to the enemy. It is living and powerful to give us victory during temptation and trial, just as our Lord Jesus Christ exemplified. *"Jesus said unto him, It is written again, Thou shalt not tempt the Lord thy God"* (Matthew 4:7). As a result, it is our sole responsibility to study God's word meditatively day and night to be able to wield the sword effectively during spiritual warfare.

Prayer: *"Praying always with all prayer and supplication in the Spirit, and watching thereunto with all perseverance and supplication for all saints… And he spake a parable unto them to this end, that men ought always to pray, and not to faint;…"* (Ephesians 6:18; Luke 18:1-7).

This refers to sacred prayers of supplication with all kinds of prayer offered in the public or privately. It could be a solemn and secret confession of sin, a request for mercy and favour or an offer of thanksgiving unto God regularly and continually. Prayer crowns every effort we make in our pilgrim journey on earth. It gives victory when the Christian soldier goes forth armed completely for spiritual war with the devil. It also helps us to keep our Christian testimony each time we overcome temptation. These prayer types are:

- Prayer of repentance and restoration – Psalm 51
- Prayer of deliverance and protection – Luke 10:17-20;
- Praying Until Something Happens (PUSH) – Luke 11:5-13; 1 Thessalonians 5:17
- Prayer of intercession and supplication – Ezekiel 22:30; 1 John 5:16
- Prayer of agreement and confrontation – Matthew 18:19
- Prayer of adoration, worship and thanksgiving – Psalm 150:6; John 11:41
- Prayer of the promises and the Word of God (praying the Scriptures) – 2 Peters 1:21
- Prayer of binding and loosing – Matthew 18:18; 12:29
- Prayer of faith – Mark 11:24; 16:17

It is important to note that all the pieces must be well guarded at any point in time in our lives. Once any of the pieces is missing, it is no longer a whole armour and danger is imminent. The Lord has promised us continuous and perpetual victory, but that is not without our own responsibilities. We are responsible to remain saints in the Lord (1 Timothy 5:22). We must be strong in the Lord (Ephesians 6:10), putting on the whole armour of God (Ephesians 6:11). We are responsible for filling ourselves with God's Word to develop our faith (Colossians 3:16). We are responsible to pray always (Luke 18:1; 1 Thessalonians 5:17).

Ignorance is not acceptable to God (Hosea 4:6; Isaiah 5:13) and it deletes those things God has appointed for us but if we faithfully and diligently do our part, God will surely never fail to fulfill His own part. He will empower the weapons in our lives and we shall win forever. Other weapons to employ are:

The Word of God: God's Word is the sword of the Spirit. (Hebrews 4:12; Jeremiah 5:14; 23:39). It has penetrating powers to cast down and probe into the realms of unseen forces. It is the harmer that breaks Satan's walls and fortifications if rightly used and applied in prayers. Feed on the Word of God. Read the Bible with passion! Internalize what you read. Devote your life to it! Ask the Holy Spirit for guidance! As you do, you will be made wiser unto understanding! "As newborn babes, desire the sincere milk of the word, that ye may grow thereby" (1 Peters 2:2). The Word of God in your heart is a threat to your challenges. Harnessing the words brings changes. Until God's words saturate your heart, mountains won't budge. Rightly claiming the Word silences barriers. So, let the Bible speak to your heart. Determine to activate it and the challenges won't stand! Sure, God's Word quickens.

Feed your mind daily with the Word of God. This daily exercise will prevent Satan from planting wrong thoughts into your mind. Entertaining wrong thoughts in the mind begins with starving the mind of the Word of God! Be informed that it is a dangerous lifestyle to adopt a carefree attitude about the Word of God as it will always prevent wrong information from filtering into your mind! Receiving and entertaining wrong information in your mind is the beginning of making wrong decisions and taking wrong steps that can lead to utter destruction!

An unguarded mind is an open doorway for all kinds of thoughts and unchecked information that can make one a pawn, a prey and a victim in the hands of Satan. Keep your heart with all diligence for out of it are the issues of life! You are to feed on the Word of God daily to avoid the infiltration of wrong information into your mind! Jesus said, man shall not live by bread alone but by every word that proceeds out of the mouth of God!

The Victory of the Cross: (1 John 3:8; Colossians 2:14-15; Ephesians 1:19-21). Jesus died on the Cross, was buried and on the third day, He resurrected from the grave. Christ's resurrection is the distinctive quality of Christianity which gives every believer a sure hope and victory because He is alive forevermore! Furthermore, He had spoilt principalities and powers (architects and builders of strongholds) on the cross when he died for our sins. There He made a public show of Satan and all his hosts.

The Blood of Jesus: (Revelation 12:11; Exodus 12:13). There is great power in the Blood of Jesus. The blood of the Lamb was a sign of victory for the children of Israel. Much more so is the blood of Jesus Christ powerfully efficacious over the strongholds of the devil, for believers. The song writer says, 'When I see the blood, I will pass over you!' You have to understand that the blood represents life. Every saved soul is redeemed through Jesus' blood. (1 Peter 2:24). By sacrificing His blood, Christ the Lamb took away our sins and sickness! Doctors claim they care but God heals. As such, Christ is the great Physician and you can be made whole by His stripes.

The Anointing of the Holy Spirit: (Isaiah 10:27; 59:19; Zechariah 4:6; Acts 10:38). It is the anointing that breaks the yoke. The Spirit of God created all things and nothing created can withstand the power of its maker. The unction or anointing is the Holy Ghost power in the name of Jesus. If these weapons are properly directed through prevailing prayers, no stronghold can stand before us as Christians. A Christian cannot pray effectively except he/she is strong in the Lord and in the power of His might by living a consistent victorious life and remains Spirit-filled. God has set us apart to be His battle axes and weapons of warfare that cannot fail (Jeremiah 1:10, 51:20).

To prevail in prayer is to be determined, resolute and importunate until the answer is secured and the yoke is broken (1 Kings 18:41-45). It is to be operated like the widow woman did, who would not give up until the unjust judge avenged her of her adversary (Luke 18:1-8). Of a truth, God is still standing and waiting to avenge for all those who will cry unto Him in prevailing prayers.

Jacob prayed prevailing prayers and overcame Esau, his life-long rival (Genesis 32:24-28). Hannah prayed the same way and secured Samuel from God (1 Samuel 1:12-18). Nehemiah prayed prevailingly and ensured the continuity of the building of the wall of Jerusalem (Nehemiah 1:4; 4:9). Daniel added fasting to prevailing prayers and receive a fruitful message for the captive Israelites in Babylon (Daniel 9:3; 10:12-14). The early church prayed and this enforced the release of Peter from Herod's grip of death (Acts 12:5, 7). Paul and Silas sought God and broke the chains and opened the prison doors (Acts 16:25-27) and the Syrophoenician woman requested importunately and obtained Christ's deliverance for her daughter (Matthew 15:21-28).

Spiritual chains and shackles can stand as delimitation to progress in life. Unless you rise up against such, you will be made a laughing stock. Never look elsewhere for spiritual help than through Christ. Deliverance is possible through spiritual weapons. Anointing breaks the yoke at the mention of the Name of Jesus. Yes, your yokes are broken this day in Jesus' Name.

Prevailing Prayers: Aspects of prevailing prayers include worship, thanksgiving, supplication, intercessions, binding and loosing and praises. It can also be strengthened and made effectual with fasting because "...this kind goeth not out but by fasting and prayers" (Matthew 17:21). Sometimes, it is prayers of praises that will cause an earthquake to destroy Satan's holds of oppressing forces, like the shout of praise brought down Jericho wall and caused every man bound to be loosed in the prison when Paul and Silas sang praises unto God (Psalms 149:6-9; Acts 16:25-27). Take time to pray. Hours of prayers must be faithfully kept. Understanding the power in prayer will spur you to pray more! The responsibility to pray rests on you if you want to be victorious. Spend more time to pray and pray without ceasing. Divine strength is possible through prayers. Always seek the face of God. Yes, prayer requires discipline, create time for it.

Make seeking God your priority every day: On daily basis, you need to have fellowship with God. Never leave home without your quiet time and family devotion. Don't be preoccupied with the affairs of this world at the expense of your soul. Always read His Word and pray to Him, Yes, make it a regular practice to seek the face of God.

Don't preempt what Jesus Christ can do for you or in your life. Everything you need is possible through Christ. He has all the power to do it. Christ is the Door to your miracle! He is the Light you need to overcome all forms of darkness. He is the great Physician that can heal all your sicknesses. Eternal and everlasting life is in Him. He is the way, the truth and the life! Master Jesus is the friend you need. He is a compassionate Pal. He is more than a friend! But you need to draw closer to Him so as to be a beneficiary of His goodness. He must know you intimately. Examine your relationship with Him. Is it cordial? Do you accept Him as your personal Saviour and Lord? If not, do something practical about it today. Remember, without Jesus, you are empty. He is all in all that you need! He has answers to all your questions. He is your hope of glory.

Do you experience any form of imprisonment - marital, mental, material and monetary? Enough of such experiences! The Lord will set you free supernaturally in Jesus' name.

Christ came to deliver you from curses of the law. He came to set you free! - totally free!! Every imprisonment you might be experiencing will bow down this day in Jesus' name! Minor or major, it is the devil that is behind all forms of imprisonment; but Jesus came to give you freedom! Be free now in Jesus' name! Also, don't give chance to the devil. Ensure you establish a strong relationship with the Lord always so that you will always enjoy His freedom. Regardless of your type of imprisonment, I pray that you will be free totally this day in Jesus' name!

Put on the whole armour of God: Use the God-given weapons in prevailing prayers and all the strongholds of opposing forces will be pulled down. You are the battle axe of the Lord. Arise! As He has said, "But he said, Yea rather, blessed are they that hear the word of God, and keep it… Wherefore the rather, brethren, give diligence to make your calling and election sure: for if ye do these things, ye shall never fall" (Luke 11:28; 2 Peter 1:10).

War against the flesh: "For the flesh lusteth against the Spirit, and the Spirit against the flesh: and these are contrary the one to the other: so that ye cannot do the things that ye would (Galatians 5:17). Furthermore, always remember that the flesh is an enemy in soul battles, divine service and the fulfillment of God's purpose for our lives. We shouldn't give it the chance to operate and control our lives' goal. Therefore:

Command your flesh to be subject to the Holy Spirit and God's laws. Bar the ways of all fleshy lusts and cravings. Tell

God to give you the grace and strength to tame your flesh, control your passions and watch your emotions. Many families have been ruined by the uncharitable use of the tongue. Pray that God will set a watch before your mouth and keep the door of your lips (Psalms 141:3).

Tell God to quicken you in righteousness, make you sensitive to holiness and dead to sin (Psalms 119:40, 159).

War against the foe! "Submit yourselves therefore to God. Resist the devil, and he will flee from you" (James 4:7). Satan is the foe. His aim is to shoot us down, halt our progress in life and ruin our peace in eternity. We shouldn't give the devil the chance to shoot at us. Alternatively, we should ensure that his shots do not hit the targets in our lives – salvation, purity, ministry, careers, children, husband and relations, among other things. We can't make peace with the devil; he won't even allow it to happen. As Christians, we have enough power to make the devil and his demons crumble like cookies. Command the devil to leave your life.

Command the devil to leave your home, parents, husband, wife and children.

Command the devil to take his ugly hands off your future. Bind all forces of darkness working against you, your family, parents, careers, ministry and general well-being.

Cast out the spirits of poverty, stagnation, barrenness, lukewarmness, accidents, sickness, marital crisis et al. I decree in Jesus name that, in your life, home and marriage, love should replace sadness and longevity would replace untimely death.

Command all-round blessings of God to be yours in the name of Jesus. Spiritual warfare is real yet you can't use Satan's weapons to fight God's battle and win! To engage the devil in warfare, you need the armours of God! Physical weapons can't fight spiritual warfare! The weapons you need are - God's word, the name of Jesus, the blood of Jesus, faith, the fire of the Holy Spirit, praise and worship, prayer! These can only work for the believers! Give thanks to God (Psalms 92:1).

Thank God for His goodness and His mercy that endures forever! Uplift His name on high as King of kings and Lord of lords! Exalt the name of the Lord and praise Him with all that are within you. Sing of His mercies which endure forever. Dance in His presence to show your total appreciation! Appreciate His goodness to you with instruments of music! Yes, praise Him and give Him glory and honour.

Worship God (Psalms 122:1). Service unto God is profitable. Undertaking in spiritual worship is worthwhile! Nothing should hinder such a moment. Devotional worship draws us closer to God and it rejoices His heart. Yes, God deserves our worship!

Showing forth God's praises (1 Peter 2:9). The Lord has performed the wonderful work of salvation in your life and you ought to express exceeding joy to Him for saving your soul! Definitely, He has done the greatest miracle-work in your life. He took away your nightmares and granted you sweet sleep! He has also performed the extraordinary in your life! So, you cannot but show forth the praises of Him Who called you out of darkness into His marvellous light! You must dedicate and surrender everything to Him. Yes, He deserves your praise.

Sing the Lord's praises aloud! (Psalms 96:8). Unto Him belongs thanks and praises! Nothing must hinder you from giving glory to God Almighty. Declare His glory, majesty and power. Adore Him with all your heart! God expects you to come to His courts with your sacrificial offerings too - Singing melodious Psalms, hymns and spiritual songs (Psalms 81:1-2; Colossians 3:16; Ephesians 5:19) Treat yourself to good music and Psalms of rejoicing. Uphold and uplift only spiritual songs; not the secular ones. Engage yourself in edifying and devotional songs! Select and use songs that please and glorify God. Divine songs and praises are good tonics for the soul. Always sing to the glory of God!

Preach the Word (2 Timothy 4:1-5). Tell the story often about how Jesus Christ came and died to save the lost. Reach souls for Christ. Sinners are about to perish. Daily carry the gospel banner to them. As Christ's ambassador, proclaim the gospel. Yes, win sinners one by one. Examine your weapons very well and ensure that they are not Satan's weapons, otherwise you will be defeated or destroyed. Mind you, spiritual warfare needs spiritual weapons. Still, you cannot use Satan's weapons to fight God's battle and win. Be holy, pure and saved. If you are a sinner, no matter how long you call the name of Jesus, like the sons of Sceva, the devil will yell or jump on you. Entering the strongman's territory requires a holy life and knowledge about the use spiritual weapons too.

Remember, the believer's weapons for warfare are not carnal instruments like candle, gun, holy water, aprons, handkerchiefs, talisman, anointing oil, incense, printed Bible or other physical materials. Whatever is your present situation, God will definitely visit you. Everything is possible with Him. Just make your requests known unto Him. None who calls on Him sincerely will be denied. Cast your cares upon Him every day. Surely, God will intervene in your matters this day in Jesus' Name. He can meet your daily needs with His divine provisions. All you need do is ask in faith. Yes, I pray for you that things would change for better in Jesus' name. In every situation, ensure to give thanks to God, more so, for the answered prayers.

SUGGESTED PRAYERS

SINS AND SALVATION

Please read: 1 Corinthians 6:9-11; Galatians 5:19-21; Psalms 51; Romans 6:23 and 1 John 1:9.

Pray thus:

Father, l have sinned against Heaven and before You, Please, have mercy and forgive me of all my sins and let the Blood of Jesus wash me and cleanse me from all sins. I confess that Jesus is the true Son of God. Lord Jesus, l accept you today as my Lord and personal Saviour. Please, come into my life, reign and save my soul from bondage of sin and from eternal damnation. Let the power to 'go and sin no more' come into my life from today. Thank you, Lord, for the answered prayers, in Jesus' mighty name I pray, Amen!

"For thou art my rock and my fortress; therefore for thy name's sake, lead me and guide me" (Psalms 31:3).

"Shew me thy ways, O LORD; teach me thy paths. Lead me in thy truth, and teach me: for thou art the God of my salvation; on thee do I wait all the day" (Psalms 25:4-5).

BREAKING THE GENERATIONAL TIDE AND SINS

Please read: Leviticus 26:40-42; Deuteronomy 5:7-10; Psalms 79:8-11; Jeremiah 32:17-18; Daniel 9:1-19; Galatians 3:12-14 and 2 Corinthians 5:15-19.

Father Lord, let the powerful Blood of Jesus Christ and the fire of Holy Ghost break all cycles of ancestral, generational and family strongholds besetting my life and frustrating my divine destiny. Let their prophecies fail over my life now in Jesus mighty name!

All generational covenants and curses as a result of the involvement of my forefathers with satanism, be broken in my life now by the powerful Blood of Jesus Christ that was shed for me on the cross. Old things are passed away in my life and I am moving from generational curses to generational blessings of Abraham through the vicarious death of Christ on the Cross in Jesus mighty name!

I renounce and loose myself from every negative evil dedication placed upon my life now in the name of Jesus. Hidden covenants, evil dedications and evil plantations against my life and progress, be uprooted and destroyed completely now in the mighty name of Jesus (Isaiah 41:7-9; Matthew 15:13).

I come against all demons associated with any broken evil parental vow and dedication, by the powerful Blood of Jesus Christ. I render you impotent and command you to depart from my life now in the Name of Jesus.

I hold the powerful Blood of Jesus Christ against all enchantments, divinations, curses, spells and evil arrows that are against directed against my life and family. I command you all destroyed now in the mighty name of Jesus (Numbers 23:23).

BREAKING THE YOKE AND THE EVIL ALTAR OF IMPRISONMENT

Please read: 1 Kings 12:9-14; Matthew 23:4; Isaiah 58:5-12; Isaiah 10:27; Psalms 107:13-14; Nahum 1:12-13; Matthew 11:28-30.

Lord Jesus! I come to You this day through the Blood You shed for me on the Cross of Calvary. Break unwanted burdens, pains, chains, curses, shackles and afflictions placed upon me by the enemy. By Your mighty power, O Lord, break the staff of the wicked and the scepter of the wicked oppressors in my life now in Jesus' mighty name! (Isaiah 14:3-5).

I cover my soul, spirit and body with the blood of Jesus Christ. O Lord! Let the Blood of Jesus Christ and the power of the Holy Ghost break every yoke on my neck that has been diverting my miracles, blessings, breakthroughs and divine elevation. I break the yoke of oppression and backwardness and all strongholds erected against my progress now in Jesus' mighty name.

O Lord my God! Let every evil and satanic altar of infirmities, sicknesses, failure, barrenness and sudden death erected against me and my family be destroyed now by the

Blood of Jesus and the fire of Holy Ghost in Jesus' name (Hebrews 12:29).

Prayers against Satan's power and his agents

Please read: Ephesians 2:4-8; 6:11-3; Colossians 2:13-15; Isaiah 54:17

I am sitting in heavenly places with Christ Jesus, I pray that God should arise and shake heaven, the whole earth, air and sea against the principalities, powers and all agents of darkness that are militating against my family. Let all satanic powers formed against my life be completely destroyed now in the name of Jesus.

Let all demonic communication networks programmed against me and my family be completely dismantled and wasted by the acidic fire of God now in Jesus' mighty name.

I bind with fetters of iron, every snake, tiger, lion, bird, lizard or any demonic being assigned to afflict me with pains and sicknesses by the authority in the name of Jesus. O Lord, I break the head of this snake (mention the demonic animals or beings that are visiting you in the dream) with Your Heavenly Rod of Iron and dash them in pieces like the potter's vessel in the mighty name of Jesus (Psalms 2:9).

"Heal me, O LORD, and I shall be healed; save me, and I shall be saved: for thou art my praise" - (Jeremiah 17:14).

All demonic invasions and monitoring spirits in my atmosphere, environments and in any area of my life, be shattered in pieces by the thunder and fire of God now in Jesus' mighty name.

I bind all satanic powers pulling my destiny towards the sun, moon or star in the Name of Jesus.

I bind every evil power and personality pulling anything in my life or body towards evil by means of energy drawn from the planets, constellations and the earth in the Name of Jesus (Matthew 18:18).

Arise, O Lord! let every witch, wizard, warlock, diviner, sorcerer and evil priest militating against my life be subdued and arrested by Holy Ghost fire now, in the Name of Jesus (Exodus 22:18).

O Lord my God and my Heavenly Father, arise and let the thunder of Heaven and Your fire locate the storehouses and strong rooms of witchcraft that are harbouring my blessings and pull them down now for my blessings to be restored in the Name of Jesus.

O Lord my God, let Your presence abide with me always. Have mercy upon me, hold my hands and go before me to open every door that the enemy has shut. Break in pieces the gate of barriers and cut in sunder the bars of iron hindering me from moving forward to my Promised Land in Jesus' mighty name (Isaiah 45:1-3).

O Lord, arise for my help and by Your mighty power, break all demonic cages and powerbases of the enemy holding my divine possession; and let my blessings be released in full to glorify your mighty name in Jesus' name (Job 20:15; Proverbs 6:31).

"But thou, O Lord, art a God full of compassion, and gracious, long suffering, and plenteous in mercy and truth. O turn unto me, and have mercy upon me; give thy strength unto thy servant, and save the son of thine handmaid. Shew me a token for good; that they which hate me may see it, and be ashamed: because thou, LORD, hast holpen me, and comforted me" (Psalms 86:15-17).

I thank You, Lord, for the answered prayers in Jesus' mighty name! Amen and Amen!!!

E-mail prayer requests and praise reports to:
akindewum@gmail.com

REFERENCES

Frederick A. Tatford (1974). *SATAN, the Prince of Darkness.* Kregel Publications, Grand Rapids, Michigan, U.S.A.

The Holy Bible (1611). *King James Version.* Trinitarian Bible Society, England (1991). (Cambridge University Press: Cambridge).

Internet Resources:

https://aminutetomidnite.com/deception-false-teaching/queen-of-heaven/

https://books.google.com.ng/books/about/SATANIC_ATTACKS_AND_THE_WAY_OUT.html?id=nMCIDwAAQBAJ&source=kp_cover&redir_esc=y

https://dictionary.cambridge.org/amp/english/manipulation

https://en.m.wikipedia.org/wiki/Psychic

http://lhfbacktobasics.weebly.com/41-the-invisible-kingdoms.html

https://science.howstuffworks.com/science-vs-myth/extrasensory-perceptions/hypnosis2.htm

https://www.amazon.com/dp/B000NN5N8S/ref=cm_sw_r_wa_apa_i_Bz4BEbT3JPDWB

https://www.biblesprout.com/articles/hell/demons/

http://www.blessedquietness,com/journal/housechu/what-satan-can-and-cannot-do.htm

https://www.express.co.uk/news/weird/1250754/ufo-sighting-iss-live-stream-nasa-anomaly-space-aliens-ancient-alien

https://www.whatchristianswanttoknow.com/sorcery-bible-definition/

www.express.co.uk

OTHER BOOKS WRITTEN BY THE AUTHOR

1. Satanic Attacks and the Way Out

2. Victorious Christian Living Essentials

3. Prevailing Prayers of Intercession and Supplication Guides

4. Satanic Attacks and the Way Out (Revised Edition)

5. Principles of Christian Marriage and Family Life.

6. Evangelization and Christian Development

These are available online with Amazon, Barnes & Nobles, Lulu Books, Blurb Publisher, Google play, Xlibris Publishers among others.